OKanaGan SLOW RoaD

WRITTEN BY BERNADETTE MCDONALD IMAGES BY KAROLINA BORN-TSCHÜMPERLIN

TouchWood
Editions

TouchWood Editions
touchwoodeditions.com

LIBRARY AND ARCHIVES CANADA CATALOGUING IN PUBLICATION
McDonald, Bernadette, 1951–, author
Okanagan slow road / written by Bernadette McDonald; images by Karolina Born-Tschümperlin.

Includes index.
Issued in print and electronic formats.
ISBN 978-1-77151-036-3

1. Okanagan Valley (BC : Region)—Guidebooks. I. Born-Tschümperlin, Karolina, 1964–, illustrator II. Title.

FC3845.O4A3 2014   917.11'5045   C2013-906761-2

Editor: Marlyn Horsdal
Proofreader: Cailey Cavallin
Design: Pete Kohut
Cover and interior images by Karolina Born-Tschümperlin unless annotated.

We gratefully acknowledge the financial support for our publishing activities from the Government of Canada through the Canada Book Fund, Canada Council for the Arts, and the province of British Columbia through the British Columbia Arts Council and the Book Publishing Tax Credit.

This book was produced using FSC®-certified, acid-free paper, processed chlorine free and printed with vegetable-based inks.

The information in this book is true and complete to the best of the author's knowledge. All recommendations are made without guarantee on the part of the author. The author disclaims any liability in connection with the use of this information.

1 2 3 4 5 18 17 16 15 14

PRINTED IN CANADA

Okanagan vineyard and lake

Contents

Okanagan sunset (photo courtesy of the McDonald collection)

After an Okanagan winter storm (photo courtesy of the McDonald collection)

Introduction

I peered out the window of the Greyhound bus. The night air was thick with snow. Enormous flakes feathered down to form an undulating blanket that enveloped the landscape, softening every edge. It was 2:00 AM when the bus rolled into Vernon, silent and stealthy on the empty white highway, the end of a journey that had begun two provinces away at my Saskatchewan boarding school. There, idling on the side of the road, was an elongated mound of snow, two black inverted triangles where the windshield wipers strained to maintain some semblance of visibility. Steam curled upward from the exhaust pipe. Inside was my dad, hunkered down in the dark, waiting for the passenger he knew would soon alight, waiting to whisk me home for the Christmas holidays.

Home. It was the first time I could call this Okanagan Valley home. My family had moved to Vernon earlier that fall, and for me, this was a great adventure. I had never seen snow like this. Feathery light. Unthinkably soft. I was accustomed to snow drifts so wind-hardened you could ride a horse across them. Now I shuffled along up to my knees in the stuff with no effort at all.

As we entered the house, a familiar aroma wrapped its arms around me—fresh baking. My mother loves to bake above all else, and there on the counter were an apple pie and a nine-by-twelve-inch pan of Rice Krispies squares. I polished off a couple of gooey squares for the main course and a juicy wedge of pie for dessert. Now I was really home.

The next day we tested that fresh blanket of snow with our new ski equipment—wooden beauties with cable bindings and supple leather boots. We marched up a hillside pasture, fumbling with the skis that refused to stay perched on our shoulders. At the top of the slope, we clamped ourselves into the bear-trap bindings and then careened down, dodging the barbed-wire fence at the bottom. No sense of style or even control.

Next to our unofficial ski hill lay a gently sloping winter orchard. Ancient, wizened apple trees stood by for the winter pruning job that

View across Okanagan Lake

I have struggled to pinpoint what makes this valley so special, and I've listened to the responses of others, both visitors and locals. Finally, I decided to try to articulate the unique qualities of the Okanagan Valley, a process that led me to other experiences in other valleys in other parts of the world, places where *slow* is a word that holds great value.

———

Slow travel: a state of mind in which the pleasure of the journey outweighs the arrival. One of the defining elements of slow travel is becoming a part of local life and connecting to a place: to its smells and tastes, to its sounds and rhythms, and, ultimately, to its people. Or as Leroy Little Bear, a Blood Indian and Harvard academic, says, "Connecting to all our relations: the people, the grass, the rocks, the animals." Slow travel builds on the Slow Food movement, which emphasizes traditional and regional cuisine. The movement is global in scope, yet rooted in individual communities and places.

would smarten them up for the spring bloom. The occasional flash of red from a forgotten apple brightened the monochrome landscape.

———

The magic of those first few days in my Okanagan home remained with me. After that first homecoming in 1967, I came and went in all seasons, for all kinds of reasons: family, work, recreation, inspiration. Skiing with my family at the Sovereign Lake cross-country area, rock climbing at the Skaha Bluffs with friends, teaching music at Okanagan College, and, finally, settling onto a piece of land with my husband and planting a small vineyard on the Naramata Bench.

This book is a languid journey through one of those places—the bucolic Okanagan Valley of south-central British Columbia. Defined by its massive lakes, the Okanagan Valley is blessed with a climate that nurtures all that lives and grows within it: from rare songbirds to Sonoran Desert antelope brush; from crisp Ambrosia apples to luscious, dripping peaches; from tart and refreshing Sauvignon Blancs to grand and complex Syrahs; from wild asparagus to mouth-watering trout. The aroma of lavender, the warm caress of the setting sun, the cool breeze off a lake, the delight of skimming through light powder snow, the melancholy call of the loon—all of these can be found in the nooks and crannies of this meandering valley. You simply need to know where to look.

This is a book that guides gently. There is no timetable. There are no GPS points. There is no tick list. There are simply experiences and images and characters, rooted in a sense of place, offered for the taking.

You don't have to be an expert to savour this valley. I am neither a food critic nor a sommelier. Neither an ornithologist nor a botanist. My partner on this journey, Karolina Born-Tschümperlin, and I admit to being unabashed amateurs, perhaps with slightly rose-tinted glasses, searching for the bewitching corners of the valley. Some of those corners are best found on a bike or in a canoe. Many are in winery tasting rooms or very special restaurants. Bakeries are a favourite, as are farmers' markets. Hiking and rock climbing are two activities that you will read a lot about. Sometimes the goal is simply to discover a perfectly formed lily or a rare woodpecker. To assist you in your search,

Gala apples "on ice"
(photo courtesy of Doug Mathias)

basic directions or street addresses can be found at the end of each chapter.

Take your time. Slow down. Taste. Smell. Listen. My hope is that the stories in this book, some of which are my own experiences, while many others come from the myriad interesting characters who live here, will inspire you to take your own voyage of discovery.

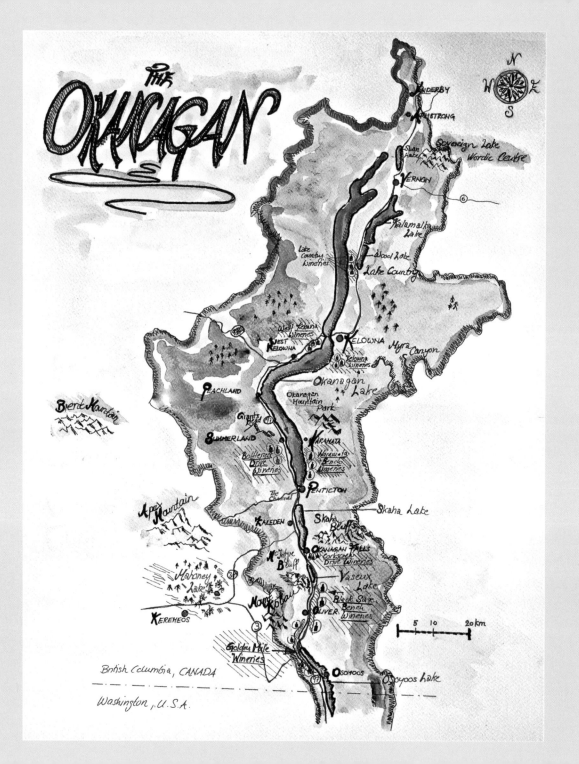

1. How Big Is the Valley?

According to Summerland author Don Gayton, the Okanagan Valley is "part urban city, part rural orchard and ranch, and part wild ponderosa pine and rock bluff."[1] That, and much more. In fact, the miracle of this expansive piece of arid real estate is water.

The valley bottom is full of it. Enormous lakes moderate the temperatures in both winter and summer, and a simple glimpse of those vast bodies of blue evokes a certain peace of mind.

The Okanagan Valley occupies a deep trench between the high, gently rolling Thompson Plateau in the west and the snowy, and more precipitous, Monashee Mountains in the east. Thirty to sixty kilometres wide and one hundred and seventy kilometres long, the valley stretches from Osoyoos in the south to Armstrong in the north. When the valley began to form, sedimentary rocks rose to the surface after millions of years of melting and hardening. Now metamorphic in nature, this gneiss is famous around the world for the high-quality rock climbing it offers. There was volcanic activity too, of which there are vivid examples throughout the valley: Munson Mountain in Penticton, Giant's Head in Summerland, Mount Boucherie near Westbank, and Knox, Dilworth, and Layer Cake Mountains in Kelowna.

It's hard to imagine a glacier filling this massive basin, but it once did that—and more. As the ice meandered south approximately two million

View from the Summerland Agricultural Research Centre

View of Okanagan Lake from above Naramata

Despite the predominance of large bodies of water, the Okanagan Valley is much more than lakes. A river also claims the valley's name. The Okanagan River rises in the northern end of the valley, near the town of Armstrong, and completes its scenic three-hundred-kilometre journey in another country, when it joins the Columbia River at Brewster, in the state of Washington. But for the most part, the Canadian portion of the Okanagan River manifests itself as a series of lakes, Kalamalka, Wood, Okanagan, Skaha, Vaseux, and Osoyoos, all linked by short stretches of the original river. The entire valley varies only slightly in elevation, from around five hundred and sixty metres above sea level at Vernon, in the northern end of the valley, to three hundred at Osoyoos, in the "deep south."

Each of the six major Okanagan lakes has a unique character. Kalamalka—Lake of Many Colours—is precisely that: a glorious kaleidoscope of hues, ranging from a deep cerulean blue to a striking aquamarine green. Wood Lake, located between Vernon and Kelowna, is a fine place to fish, particularly for kokanee salmon. Skaha Lake has a restless, choppy character, as it provides a direct funnel for the north-south blows so common in the southern part of the valley. But it's also a lake of spectacular beaches. The beach at its southern end occupies one entire boundary of the town of

years ago, it grew to a depth of two kilometres and finally overflowed the edges of the valley. One of the remnants of this ice sheet was instrumental in creating the lakes that now fill the valley floor. In the South Okanagan, the looming cliffs above Vaseux Lake form the narrowest part of the valley. It was here that a titanic chunk of glacier created a solid, icy plug. Behind the plug, the Okanagan River, which was by that time flowing freely from the north, got backed up and formed a lake that filled the valley all the way to Enderby, one hundred and seventy kilometres away. For a time, the river changed direction, flowing north out of this new body of water, which was called Lake Penticton. But eventually the glacial plug melted and the river resumed its southerly course.

Okanagan Lake on a winter's day

Okanagan Falls, and an even larger beach at its northern end forms the southern boundary of Penticton, a community that calls itself the City of Peaches and Beaches. Vaseux is a birder's lake, and the quietest of the bunch, since no motorboats are allowed. Osoyoos is a lake of the south, which has the feel of a desert. But of all the lakes that grace this pastoral valley, Okanagan is the queen. One hundred and thirty-five kilometres long, with depths that reach two hundred and thirty metres, it stretches all the way from Penticton to Vernon. It dominates and defines the valley and is perhaps its greatest resource.

The region boasts four distinct ecosystems: narrow ribbons of dry grassland on the benchlands on either side of the valley bottom; coniferous forests that stretch to the mountaintops; islands of alpine tundra that cap the highest peaks; and lakes, rivers, marshes, and other water-rich habitats.

Because of its unique climate, the Okanagan Valley is bursting with riches and claims an impressive diversity of plants and animals, many of which are not found anywhere else in Canada. More than two hundred bird species nest in the many distinct valley zones: alpine birds, coastal birds, desert birds, and forest birds. Considered the most northerly extension of the great Sonoran Desert, which begins thousands of kilometres farther south in Northwest Mexico, the Okanagan Valley has places where desert sands blow in the hot afternoon winds and rattlesnakes slither among the rocky cliffs and grasslands. Merely a few kilometres away, with a rise in altitude, meadows lie smothered in alpine flowers and stunted trees cling to the ridgelines, braced against the ceaseless cold winds.

Because the valley lies in the rain shadow of

Apple blossom time

the Cascades and the Coast Mountains to the west, where most of the storms originate, there is very little precipitation. The South Okanagan is the driest part of the valley, receiving only about thirty centimetres of precipitation each year. At the valley's northern limit at Armstrong, the annual precipitation rises to forty-five centimetres and the vegetation responds accordingly: Armstrong is a greener shade of green.

The annual parade of the seasons is a miracle in all regions of the country, but it marches to a slightly different rhythm in the Okanagan. Spring arrives early, with the first sagebrush buttercups and yellow bells and the migrating birds that move up from the southern states in late February. By late March the orchards begin to bloom. Acres upon acres of white and pink and peach blossoms fill the valley with a froth of pastels. The warm days are gentle and the cool nights refresh. By the end of June, however, the hot, arid winds are flowing up from the Great Basin Desert in the south, saturating the valley with the heat required to ripen all those peaches and grapes. Autumn is a welcome reprieve from the summer heat and brings cooler nights, golden aspens, and another flood of birds, this time winging south. Winter seeps in slowly, usually accompanied by a maddening valley fog that obscures the blue skies overhead. When snow does fall, it's up on the mountaintops where, high above the fog, the sun dazzles and the skiing is superb!

Okanagan Lake and Munson Mountain on a stormy summer's evening (photo courtesy of the McDonald collection)

The Okanagan climate is actually rather harsh, but not because of the winters. It's the summers that tax the natural world to its very limit. Spring is the season of growth, but when the hot summer winds scour the valley, the ponderosa pines, shrubs, and grasses retreat into a kind of holding pattern, guarding what little moisture they've absorbed, waiting for the cooler temperatures of fall.

This unique climate means the Okanagan Valley has the greatest concentration of species at

Winter in the valley (photo courtesy of Verena Frick)

Pussy willow buds just about to break open

risk in the entire country. Here you can find four-teen kinds of bats as well as spadefoot toads, rubber boas, scorpions, black widow spiders, rattlesnakes, and many, many more. Canyon wrens and sage thrashers live only in the most southerly reaches of the Okanagan Valley, as does the dainty and exquisite mariposa lily. The first explanation for the plethora of threatened species is that these flora and fauna are rare in Canada, due to the country's harsh climate. It is only down in this southern hotspot that they can survive, and even thrive.

The second reason is habitat loss: it's not only wild things that love this place. Many swamps and grasslands and seemingly useless piles of rock, all of which host important species of flora and fauna, are being replaced by roads and condos and big box stores for the steady influx of people. In 2013, when the *Huffington Post* declared the Okanagan Valley the number one wine-tasting area in the world to visit, it became obvious that creating a balance between development and preservation would be a challenge.

Apricot tree in bloom

Haynes Point Provincial Park

2. A Northern Desert

The southernmost section of the Okanagan Valley is unique in Canada, for it offers a landscape normally found only much farther south. The Great Basin is a large biome (a geographical region containing a certain community of flora and fauna) that includes Nevada, eastern Oregon, parts of Idaho, and some of the Washington State portion of the Columbia Basin. Low elevations, hot, dry summers, mild winters, and low precipitation define this immense stretch of country. The iconic symbol of the Great Basin is the Wyoming big sagebrush, a gnarled, grey-bearded shrub that twists and turns its way to nearly tree size. Very interesting, you might say, but what does this have to do with the Okanagan? In fact, a great deal, because immediately south of the Canadian border the northern edge of the Great Basin splits into two northward-reaching arms, one of which is the southern Okanagan Valley. The area near Osoyoos is one of only two Canadian examples of this ecological phenomenon. (The other is the Similkameen Valley, west of the Okanagan.)

Annual rainfall in the South Okanagan is similar to that in southern Arizona, which might explain why so many Canadians from other provinces migrate here each year. Amid the prevalent sagebrush, which carpets the rolling hillsides, there is an even ganglier shrub, its rambling branches looking like survivors of a not-too-recent fire. This is the famous antelope brush, found only in the most southerly regions. Often seen growing next to the antelope brush is the small red three-awn grass. Their partnership represents one of the rarest plant groupings in the entire country. Along with these two are prickly pear cacti and bunchgrasses, green in the spring and golden all summer long.

In the late 1960s and early 1970s, I commuted from my home in the North Okanagan to university in Washington State, which meant passing through the South Okanagan several times a year. The valley bottom was filled with orchards and market gardens but the hillsides were empty. At least that's what I thought. I knew nothing about sagebrush or antelope brush or bunchgrass groupings. Nor did I understand why they are important, that they provide essential habitat for birds like sage thrashers and desert sparrows that depend on these very shrubs and grasses for their existence.

As the sagebrush is the king of shrubs in this part of the valley, so the ponderosa pine is the emperor of trees. Majestic. Tall. Elegant. Its long, slender needles whisper a mysterious murmur in the summer winds. Ponderosa pines are remarkably tolerant to drought and high temperatures, but they are not immune to the ravages of the most intense forest fires or the horrific onslaught of the pine beetle. The southern ponderosa pine forests are still somewhat intact, but it may be only a matter of time before the pine beetle arrives.

Haynes Point, looking toward the United States border

While some birds rely on the sagebrush meadows, others flock to the ponderosa forests. Tiny, industrious pygmy nuthatches scurry up and down the furrowed red bark of ponderosa pines, searching for insects. And it's among those lofty branches that the rare and strikingly patterned white-headed woodpecker is sometimes spied, his ruby-red eye patch flashing in the sun.

As the elevation increases, the open, grassy ponderosa pine forests make way to stately Douglas firs, which in turn give way to Engelmann spruce, lodgepole pines, western larches, and even subalpine firs up in the highest regions. Back down in the valley bottom, clustered along the lakeshores and crowding the creek drainages, are willow, aspen, and black cottonwood trees.

Haynes Point Provincial Park is one of the most southerly spots in the valley. So close to the United States border that you can almost see the border guards, Haynes Point is a long, slender pencil of land that juts out into Osoyoos Lake and culminates in a sandbar that reaches almost to the opposite shore. It's allegedly British Columbia's most in-demand campground, and almost every single site has its own private beach! Equally appealing is a small trail system that meanders through a wetland area next to the campground. As soon as you drop down into the marsh, you will discover that the air resonates with birdsong: the

Desert Cultural Centre at Nk'Mip Cellars Winery

piercing sounds of female blackbirds defending their nests; the distinctive songs of marsh wrens bustling about, building their tiny shelters; the melodious tremolo of yellow warblers, trilling as only warblers can.

In the town of Osoyoos, you can begin to get a sense of this watery landscape, where Highway 3 crosses Osoyoos Lake at its narrowest point. Here is a place to stop and gaze. And listen. Between the months of October and April, the lake is an important migratory resting stop; it is also a wintering ground for waterfowl. The lake teems with life and the highway bridge provides an ideal viewpoint, particularly early in the morning before the traffic picks up.

Continuing east on Highway 3, up a series of heart-stopping switchbacks (in a car) and lung-expanding turns (on a bike), you'll gain almost one thousand metres of elevation before reaching Anarchist Mountain (also known as Anarchist Summit), one of the boundaries of the Okanagan Valley. To the east is the entrance to the Kettle

Mount Kobau (photo courtesy of the McDonald collection)

River drainage basin. But to the west, looking out from any of the many pull-offs along the road, is a stunning, airy view of the Okanagan Valley.

Back down at the bottom of the hill, immediately after you re-enter Osoyoos, is an Okanagan—and Aboriginal—success story. Nk'Mip Cellars Winery is blessed with twelve hundred acres of prime grape-growing land on the Black Sage Bench, all within their territory. This land produces some of the highest quality grapes in the Okanagan Valley. But it's more than grapes and wine at Nk'Mip. You can feel the difference as soon as you arrive. The architecture, the landscape, the Desert Cultural Centre. Nk'Mip is permeated by connection—a fundamental sense of place.

Across the valley is 1,863-metre Mount Kobau, which offers one of the best panoramas of the entire valley. The journey to the peak of Mount Kobau begins at the top of Richter Pass, the height of land between Osoyoos and Keremeos. It's a gentle and unimpressive mountain pass, although I'm sure the Ironman competitors who used to slog up the pass on the bike leg of their race would disagree. The nineteen-kilometre gravel road that heads up from Richter Pass is something quite different: steep, rough, and loose.

I managed to overheat the motor on the ascent and completely destroy a tire on the way down. Still, it was worth it. Driving up that winding road, watching the contours of the valley become fainter with each turn, climbing past the cultivated farms, through the desert landscape, then the Douglas fir forest, and finally out onto the open slopes of the rolling alpine meadows, you make a trip through ecological time. The haze and dust obscure the distant valley until it is merely a series of interlocking curves, overlapping and connecting, like shimmering waves, for as far as the eye can see. Directly overhead, the sky is clearer and a rich, deep blue—like an alpine sky. The heat dissipates and the air becomes cool and fresh, with a light breeze.

A short one-kilometre stroll from the summit parking lot leads to the old fire lookout, which, not surprisingly, offers a panoramic view down into the valley: to Osoyoos, straight below; north to Oliver and McIntyre Bluff; west to the imposing mountains above Keremeos; down to the US border in the south; and all the way to Mount Baldy in the east. Endless, high, rolling grassland, much of which forms a patchwork quilt of semi-protected areas.

Mount Kobau is the largest of four unconnected sites that form the South Okanagan Grasslands Protected Area, and is the source of seven creeks that flow into the Okanagan and Similkameen Rivers. The plant community on the upper slopes is red-listed, signifying that it is at risk. When you examine the details of this landscape, you can see some remarkable interfaces. Alpine flowers growing next to desert flowers. Alpine hermit thrushes flitting around with Brewer's sparrows, which are usually found in deserts. Alpine fir growing next to sagebrush. The incongruities are repeated over and over.

As I wandered along the trail to the fire lookout, puzzling at this somewhat confusing mix of species, a pair of red-tailed hawks soared overhead, dipping and diving in the updraft rushing up from the Testalinden drainage. As they disappeared from sight, a family of ravens took their place, appearing to have equal fun playing in the wind.

A second loop trail, four kilometres in length, wanders off the summit and down to Testalinden Lake. And yet a third option exists, heading north, gradually descending over the ridgetops, all the way to—where? I have yet to discover the end of this hike, several hours away, where a drop-off vehicle is required. Save that one for another day.

Mount Kobau is also Canada's premier astronomical observatory site, due to the clarity of the air and the absence of artificial light. It has been declared a Dark Sky Preserve—a place to spend the evening with a good telescope. In fact, hundreds of amateur astronomers flock here every August for the Mount Kobau "star party," which features lectures, competitions, and stargazing. The ideal Mount Kobau expedition would include an afternoon hike complete with flower sniffing and birdwatching, a leisurely picnic finished off with chilled local wine, a spectacular sunset, and some serious stargazing as the night sky closes in.

There is one more visual treat on this little excursion. Back down near Highway 3, immediately below Richter Pass and tucked into a fold in the hills, is a very odd body of water. Called Spotted Lake, it is exactly that. The shapes and shades of the white-edged ovals that cover the lake

Spotted Lake (photo courtesy of the McDonald collection)

like an abstract painting are mesmerizing. And enticing. Even more so because access to the lake is prohibited by the local First Nations on whose land it exists. They consider Kliluk, as they call it, sacred. The strange-looking circles are actually Epsom salts, caused by the periodic flooding and drying of this alkaline pond. As I stood there, staring, trying to understand the science, a stately heron picked its way across one of the white salty bits.

⁓

The highway leads back down to the northern end of Osoyoos, where the Osoyoos Desert Centre offers a superb introduction to the area, including details of the flora and fauna that inhabit this northern desert. Perhaps one of the most important stops to make to understand the delicate balance in the southern Okanagan ecosystem, the nature interpretive facility and research centre is open from May to October. The one-and-a-half-kilometre elevated boardwalk is an easy jaunt, with self-guided or guided options, both of which leave you more appreciative of the subtleties of the landscape. And that's one of the important keys to understanding this landscape. It's not garish or brightly coloured or lush. Instead, the colours are soft and understated. It is a highly specialized and adapted ecology that is tough, resilient, and worth protecting. Learning to identify the vesper

A "pic-a-nic" basket

sparrows, lark sparrows, calliope hummingbirds, western bluebirds, sagebrush, rabbitbrush, antelope brush, desert flowers, and many graceful desert grasses takes some time. It takes a slow approach. And patience.

At the north end of Osoyoos Lake, a trail system leads through an oxbow area that teems with migratory and resident birds. Tucked up next to the canal that feeds into Osoyoos Lake is the beginning of the International Hiking and Biking Trail. This is where we begin our journey north, albeit with countless detours and stops along the way.

Nk'Mip Cellars Winery
1400 Rancher Creek Road
Osoyoos, BC

Mount Kobau
Drive west from Osoyoos on Highway 3 to the top of the hill (Richter Pass). Immediately past a gravel pit, turn right up a gravel road. Continue for 19 km to the trailhead parking lot. This excursion is best enjoyed over an entire day. No point in rushing back down to the valley.

Osoyoos Desert Centre
14580 146th Avenue
Osoyoos, BC
To really enjoy the desert centre, and to get the most out of its interpretive displays, a couple of morning hours would be the right amount of time to spend here.

The Sonora Room Restaurant at
Burrowing Owl Estate Winery

3. The Black Sage Bench

It is hard to imagine a region more focused on grapes than the Black Sage Bench. Situated on the eastern side of the South Okanagan Valley, it is north of Osoyoos and across from the Golden Mile. One of the bench's best attributes is that you can get to it from the south without ever turning the key to your car. A bike trail heads out of north Osoyoos and continues up along the canal to Black Sage Road, which runs the length of the bench. No pesky traffic lights, no cars whizzing by—simply a relaxing, level bike trail, the canal on one side, fields and pastures on the other. As you climb up from the canal trail to the slightly elevated Black Sage Bench, you will be surrounded by some of the best red wine grapes in all of Canada. The sandy soil, combined with extreme afternoon heat, produces the lush big reds that the Okanagan is starting to be known for: Syrah, Merlot, and Cabernet Sauvignon.

One of the best-known wineries along this bench is Burrowing Owl Estate Winery. The owners, Jim and Midge Wyse, began their love affair with owls when they purchased a vineyard near Osoyoos and chose to name it after the endangered bird. Now, in addition to making superb wine, they support research on burrowing owls and are committed to being as green as possible. Their cellar is built deep into a hillside—they rely on the earth itself to maintain a stable environment in which to age their wines without electricity.

Burrowing Owl has so many good qualities it's hard to know where to begin. The Southwest-style, multi-storey winery and adjoining guest house and tasting room are impressive. They somehow manage to achieve an imposing stature while maintaining the casualness of adobe architecture. Climbing to the top of the winery tower and ringing the bell is a must. But standing quietly up in that airy perch and surveying the enormous scale of this productive bench, with bone-dry hills hovering over the vineyards and blue mountains shimmering in the distance—that is pure magic.

The Sonora Room Restaurant is one of the top winery dining rooms in the Okanagan Valley. Inside, or out on the wraparound balcony, the cuisine, created with care by executive chef Chris Van Hooydonk, is splendid. I usually stop in for lunch, but I finally succumbed to their five-course dinner, which, when paired with their superb wines, left me reeling.

Burrowing Owl produces consistently high-quality wines, winning lots of awards, but their Syrah is exceptional. It's dark and plummy, with hints of other mysteries: a touch of black cherry, a wee bit of blackberry, even pepper and vanilla.

Balcony at Burrowing Owl Estate Winery

This is a complex wine that is beautifully balanced and oh so big.

———

A completely different scene exists across the road at Black Hills Estate Winery. Stylish, urban, and chic—that's the overwhelming impression you get when you approach this ultra-modern building.

It wasn't always like that. Black Hills Estate Winery was once a quaint Quonset hut plunked down in the middle of their vineyard. The modest and technologically limited facility was a landmark on the Black Sage Road wine trail for years, renowned for both its humble character and the Sorry, Sold Out sign usually mounted outside.

Black Hills is something of a celebrity winery, a rarity in the Okanagan Valley. One of the owners is actor Jason Priestley, and their Nota Bene wine is one of the legendary—almost cult—wines of the Okanagan. Although Nota Bene was developed by winemaker Senka Tennant, who now owns her own establishment up on the Naramata Bench, current Black Hills winemaker Graham Pierce is committed to the same painstakingly exact vinification techniques that have been employed since the winery's first vintage in 1999. This includes practices such as "über-gentle" handling of the grapes at crush time, choosing appellation-specific oak barrels from select coopers, and continuous,

Black Sage Bench

Entrance to Black Hills Estate Winery

a sommelier, and the objective is to taste—and learn about—the wines. Black Hills is one of only two Okanagan growers of Carmenère, the grape that almost disappeared in France and was resurrected in South America. But the crème de la crème of their selection is obvious: the Bordeaux-style blend of Cabernet Sauvignon, Merlot, and Cabernet Franc—the famous, the one and only, Nota Bene (which means "take note" in Latin). It's impossible to ignore this wine. The tasting experience starts at your nose, with the seductive aromas of plum and cassis. Moving on to that first tentative sip, you notice a certain richness and complexity: there is black cherry and strawberry, maybe even a hint of dark chocolate. This wine is very balanced and silky, and the finish is long and smooth. They suggest cellaring it, which makes a lot of sense, but takes great self-discipline!

The classy, understated style at Black Hills extends out through the large windows and glass doors to the patio and pool beyond. This is a place to reflect and relax. To enjoy the glorious view across the valley to the Golden Mile—another wine-growing area—and to summon up the energy to get back on that bike and continue up the valley.

⦿

There are several more wineries between Black Hills and the northern end of Black Sage Road.

obsessive monitoring of the progress of each barrel of wine in the cellar.

Sampling is a different experience at Black Hills. They call it "slow" tasting. Unlike most tasting rooms, where you stand at the bar, here you sit at a table on which a gleaming row of appropriate glasses awaits, along with a crisp notepad and very sharp pencil. The tasting is facilitated by

Rose garden at Silver Sage Winery

It's only a matter of stamina. One of the more unusual wines I've tasted was at Silver Sage Winery, north of Black Hills. Called Sage Grand Reserve, this wine is basically a Gewürztraminer, which, under normal circumstances, is an easy-drinking, spicy white. But this one has something different—something more aromatic. Sage! Their version of Gewürztraminer is fermented with wild sage, which produces a completely different and unique aroma and taste.

The other surprise at Silver Sage is the landscaping outside the winery. Unlike most wineries, which go in for the xeriscape look, Silver Sage has one of the most traditional-looking, luxurious rose gardens in the entire valley. Wandering among these deep red, precious pink, and pale peach beauties is to be transposed back in time. You almost want a cup of tea!

Burrowing Owl Estate Winery
500 Burrowing Owl Place
Oliver, BC

Black Hills Estate Winery
4318 Black Sage Road
Oliver, BC

Silver Sage Winery
4852 Ryegrass Road RR1
Oliver, BC

Miradoro Restaurant at Tinhorn Creek Vineyards

4. The Golden Mile and a Church

The Golden Mile was one of the first clearly defined winery areas of the South Okanagan. The name works on several levels. It is a marketing tool and a geographical delineation, but, most importantly, it is a definition of soil and elevation. The Golden Mile wineries are on the west side of the valley, north of Osoyoos, on an elevated bench on the lower slopes of Mount Kobau. The bench is composed almost exclusively of rocky and gravelly loam, a condition of soil created as the mountain crumbles its way to the valley floor below. Facing east, the Golden Mile basks in gentle morning light and then escapes into shadows during the hot late-afternoon hours. Here, on this well-drained stretch of terroir, it is white grapes that grow best: Gewürztraminer, Pinot Gris, Viognier, Muscat, and Chardonnay.

One of the Golden Mile wineries is Tinhorn Creek. As I wandered up through their extensive vineyards en route to the Golden Mile Stamp Mill Trail, I was astonished by the scale of the Gewürztraminer and Viognier plantings, both signature Tinhorn wines. Their red wines are made from grapes sourced from vineyards directly across the valley on the Black Sage Bench, which, because it faces due west and is at a lower elevation, bakes in the late-afternoon sun, producing those big, sweet, juicy red berries.

Named after the creek that runs through the property, Tinhorn Creek Vineyards is both aware and respectful of its wild surroundings. "As farmers we were stewards of the land," says Kenn Oldfield, chairman and owner of Tinhorn Creek. "This means the natural areas around our farms, as well as the vineyards that give us the wine." Their numerous initiatives include antelope brush habitat restoration, snake fencing, and an invasive-weed management program. The snake fence is a curious construction—low to the ground and made of small-diameter mesh, it is apparently quite effective at keeping rattlesnakes out of the vineyard.

Oldfield is an interesting character who has led Tinhorn Creek since its inception in 1994. Originally from the Muskoka District of Ontario, he moved to Alberta, worked for fourteen years in the oil industry, and then turned his attention to a new venture—Tinhorn Creek Vineyards. But he didn't do so blindly. He armed himself with a master's degree in viticulture from the University of California, Davis, before beginning the huge task of planting one hundred and fifty acres of vineyard land, and building a winery, an outdoor amphitheatre, and a barrel cellar.

Tinhorn Creek is a handsome winery, with a modern architectural style, wonderful views of the valley below, and some special touches that make it stand out. One that has always impressed me is the miniature vineyard laid out in front of the winery—precise little rows, meticulously pruned and tended, carefully labelled so that you can identify each varietal, and anchored at each end with a luxuriously blooming rose bush. It is both educational and exquisite in its symmetry.

Tinhorn Creek also hosts a concert series on the fourth Saturday of each month, May through September. Yes—music in the vineyard. No, you don't have to sit on the ground, fighting off rattlers and scorpions. Not at all. Simply settle into the amphitheatre, open up your picnic, take a sip of one of the wines on offer, and enjoy the music. Their website is the best place to get the latest info on their Canadian Concert Series. Not only can you see who is playing, but you can also listen to a clip of the music.

I'm not an expert, but if I had to choose one wine to sip while enjoying a concert at Tinhorn, it would be their Oldfield Series Syrah. The Oldfield Series consists of winemaker Sandra Oldfield's signature wines, and her Syrah is made from grapes grown in both their Golden Mile Bench vineyards and their Diamondback vineyards across the valley on the Black Sage Bench. Dark and plum-coloured, this Syrah is full-bodied, with hints of pepper and all kinds of leathery, earthy, raisin, and currant characteristics. This is a big, luscious wine.

If a picnic is not your style, there is another option. The Miradoro Restaurant, with its panoramic views of the South Okanagan Valley, overlooks many of the farms that supply the ingredients used in the kitchen. The Mediterranean-influenced menu is rustic, creative, and very seasonal. As my husband and I settled into our chairs on their elevated deck and gazed across the valley, a cool breeze slipped down from the hills above the winery and a refreshing mist caressed our faces—yes, mist! The restaurant has mounted misters under the spectacular overhanging roof to cool diners on hot afternoons. The entire situation is quite dramatic: cantilevered about eight metres above the abyss, the outdoor eating area is angular and clean and surrounded by expansive glass balcony borders to ensure an unobstructed view. It feels airy—but is perhaps not the best choice for someone with a fear of heights. This is a classy place, but, as at almost every classy restaurant in the Okanagan, you can arrive by limo, on your bike, or on foot. A little sweat and dust are de rigueur here. Casual elegance.

We sampled a simple but yummy flatbread quattro formaggi pizza. With its thin crust and rich cheesy toppings, it paired beautifully with Tinhorn Creek's 2Bench white blend. In complete contrast, the penne we tasted had an unusual lemony mint sauce and was studded with fresh peas. Miradoro's chef, Jeff Van Geest, has studied and worked in some of the most prestigious establishments in the country and is most respected for his commitment to modern, local, and sustainable cuisine. I was impressed with his creativity.

Now that the tummies are full, it's time for a little hike. Luckily, you don't have to go far. The Golden Mile trail heads straight up from the winery, past the somewhat intimidating snake fence, and on to the lower slopes of Mount Kobau. The views are superb: Mount Baldy to the east, the town of Oliver to the north, Osoyoos Lake to the south, and the orderly vineyards of the Black Sage Bench directly across the valley. Right below you, looking rather small now, is Tinhorn Creek Vineyards. As the trail winds back across Tinhorn Creek, a small, partially shaded meadow provides a cozy spot for a picnic or a post-lunch nap and

Tinhorn Creek winery building (right) and Miradoro (left)

is the site of the historic, one-hundred-year-old Tinhorn Creek stamp mill ruins. The trail continues south across the creek to more Golden Mile wineries situated on the bench.

One of these is Hester Creek. Tranquil and romantic—these are the words most often used to describe Hester Creek Estate Winery. Reminiscent of a scene in Italy, the patio at Hester Creek is bordered by soaring pillars and a grapevine-draped arbour. The smooth, mustard-hued walls provide an elegant contrast to the wood-framed French doors and dark iron light fixtures.

But the pièce de résistance is found at the edge of the patio: the thickly gnarled, forty-year-old trunks of those very vines that protect the patio from the blazing Okanagan sun. With lavender blooming out front, the Merlot block just beyond, and a glass of Cabernet Franc in hand, what could be more relaxing than sitting here?

It's difficult to leave that patio, but if you must,

Wine shop at Hester Creek Estate Winery

make it for lunch inside at Terrafina Restaurant. Terrafina—the word means "from the earth"— uses the guiding principle of Tuscan food: few ingredients but of the very best quality, all locally sourced. Yet Chef Jeremy Luypen's lighthearted sensibility shows in the changeable and eclectic menu. House-made pastrami is piled high, then loaded with oozing buffalo mozzarella, the rich sandwich offset by a peppery arugula salad. Thin crust pizzas are topped with roasted eggplant, zucchini, and mushrooms, all imbued with a rustic, smoky taste from the wood-burning oven. Although the restaurant offers wines from a number of local wineries, Hester Creek's Character Red—a Bordeaux blend—is a good match for the earthy flavours of these lunchtime choices.

This is one of the best winery restaurant experiences in the Okanagan, one that is complemented by the view and the ambience. When you are pining away for Italy, this is the place to come.

The food is uncomplicated, unpretentious, locally sourced, flavourful, and ample, and is served in a friendly manner and in a lovely setting. Co-owner April Goldade calls it "upscale, casual dining," and I would be inclined to agree.

⚜

The nearby town of Oliver calls itself the Wine Capital of Canada. Maybe so, but I think they also have one of the most original coffee shops in Canada. Located in what was formerly a church, Medici's Gelateria and Coffee House lives at peace with the higher forces in a roomy, almost cavernous structure, now painted a striking blue. Inside the coffee house and on one of its soaring towers, gigantic murals grace the walls. One depicts a landscape that looks remarkably like Lugano, Switzerland. Former church pews provide the seating, and a funky upright piano holds a place of pride on a small stage. Why is there a piano in the coffee house? For music, obviously. In the traditional coffee-house style, this place isn't merely about eating and drinking; it is also a community gathering place.

Apart from the setting, the luscious gelato is the prime attraction. Swirls of deep pink gelato, studded with fresh raspberries. Deep coral piles of the stuff, topped with fresh mango. Pale yellow scoops, decorated with slices of orange. Beautiful to look at. Fresh and rich and mouth-wateringly tasty.

Fresco of Lake Lugano, Switzerland, at Medici's Gelateria and Coffee House in Oliver

Their ample parking affords another great option for this southern Okanagan town. Park the car and hop on the bike. The back streets and side roads of Oliver and its region are home to some of the most intensive market gardening and orcharding around. The narrow roads are almost deserted, except for the occasional tractor. Pedalling along on a bike is a much more civilized way to inspect those juicy cherries, deep red tomatoes ripening on the vines, and myriad peppers—black, red, yellow, and green—maturing week by week. Many roads are dead ends, but it really doesn't matter. Beans and squash and apples and apricots. Row upon row of fresh produce, some of it available as u-pick, but if not, there is always a fruit-and-vegetable stand nearby. This is serious food-production country, and sometimes it seems almost a miracle that it has remained that way. Not a condo in sight. This is a place to marvel at the beauty of a perfectly formed red pepper and fully understand the concept of field to table.

Tinhorn Creek Vineyards
32830 Tinhorn Creek Road
Oliver, BC

Hester Creek Estate Winery
877 Road 8
Oliver, BC
The Golden Mile Stamp Mill Trail can be as short or as long as you make it. Combined with tastings and lunch at the wineries, it makes for a lovely day.

Medici's Gelateria and Coffee House
9932 350th Avenue
Oliver, BC

McIntyre Bluff, south of Okanagan Falls

5. McIntyre Bluff Hike and Covert Farms

Imagine ascending a mountain made of rock that is two billion years old. That is the case with McIntyre Bluff, the prominent prow that thrusts into the narrowest stretch of the Okanagan Valley between Oliver and Okanagan Falls. But it's entirely possible to get to the top of this impressive chunk of rock—from the back. A sparsely signed hiking trail that begins at the back end of Covert Farms leads up through open sage and antelope brush grasslands, then ponderosa pine forests, and finally to the top of the precipitous bluff. The hardest part is finding the trail.

Turning west off Highway 97, Secrest Hill Road winds up a series of turns, past a garlic farm and some vineyards, before reaching Covert Farms. The six-hundred-acre establishment, which includes vegetable gardens, berry patches, vineyards, and a winery, is perched on a kame terrace above the main Okanagan Valley. Kame terraces are massive deposits of sand and gravel left by meltwater streams that once flowed between the glacial ice and the valley walls. They are usually found along the side of a glaciated valley, as in the case of Covert Farms.

But you still need to find the trail! Upon arriving at the farm, continue driving past the well-signed market, then through what appears to be an industrial yard crowded with antique farm machinery. Follow the u-pick berry signs straight toward a steep, grassy slope that lies behind a three-metre-high deer fence. Here you will find a narrow gate with a sign announcing the McIntyre Bluff trail. The trail initially hugs the electrified deer fence, before breaking free and beginning its climb up the slope. After about twenty minutes of hiking, it's worth taking a short break to gaze back at the rows and rows of vines and begin to grasp the scale of the Covert Farms vineyards and the kame terrace on which they are planted. Massive. And very flat.

But the vineyards are not the point of this hike. The steepening slope is blanketed in classic grasslands flora that, depending on the season, can be exquisite. In May the shaggy, forlorn-looking antelope brush are smothered in tiny

"Strawberry Fields Forever" at Covert Farms

a mountain bike most of the way, with only these last steep bits off limits. The top of McIntyre is actually quite dramatic, as it drops away—three hundred metres—straight down to the valley bottom. Every time I come up here, I can't resist checking around very carefully to ensure that I'm not about to sit on a dozing snake. It would be such a shame to run the wrong way!

After an arid hike up the bluff, you deserve a visit to the Covert Farms Market and tasting room. The farm itself is a complicated affair. In fact, there is so much to do (and sample) at Covert Farms, it is hard to do it all in one day. For starters, there are the berry patches. Tucked in at the back of the farm, dozens of rows of blueberries march toward the hills leading up to McIntyre Bluff. Some bushes are tall and elegant, while others are short and squat, but all are laden with hundreds and thousands of deep blue, juicy orbs of goodness.

Morning is the best time to pick, before it gets too hot. This is an organic farm and it's soon apparent what this means: no herbicides or chemicals. Each weed is removed by hand. The neighbouring trees swarm with songbirds that warble along while you pick. A cool breeze refreshes—at least for the first hour. But by mid-morning it's getting steamy and it's time to weigh the pails. I picked ten pounds of berries—ideal

yellow blossoms. Long-leafed phlox bloom in the millions, their dainty, pale pink petals a stylish match for the silvery sage among which they nestle. Wild blue flax wave in the breeze, while purple daisies, yellow paintbrush, and prickly pear cacti strut their colours. Out here in the open grasslands, meadowlarks sing their hearts out, and farther along, where the trail dips in among aspen groves and towering ponderosa pines, you can hear American goldfinches and flickers.

Occasional trail signs show the way, past Rattlesnake Lake (I've never seen one here, although I was once almost trampled by a herd of stampeding cattle), down through a couple of steep-sided, shady gullies, and finally up the last remaining barren slopes to the rocky summit. You can ride

for freezing. There is nothing as mouth-watering and evocative of summer as a few frozen blueberries popped into a bowl of steaming hot porridge on a frosty winter morning. As the little berries thaw, oozing into the oatmeal and yogurt, an ordinary breakfast suddenly becomes gourmet, and a vision of that steamy, summery blueberry patch floats into view.

Next to the blueberry patch is the blackberry patch. And beyond that, the tomato fields. And even farther, the squash field, the cucumbers, and the beets. A paradise of fresh fruits and vegetables.

Now it's time to sample what the market has to offer. Positioned near the entrance to the farm, this shed-like building is bustling the day I visit. Kids everywhere! "What's going on?" I ask Chef Derek Uhlemann, who seems to have half a dozen of them behind the counter, peeling and stirring and cooking. He explains that this is the second-last day of the Young Organic Farmers Camp. Owner Shelley Covert teaches the kids everything from composting to differentiating good bugs from bad bugs to intercropping. After she's finished with all the useful agricultural tips, Uhlemann shows them how to cook. That explains why they're behind the counter. He nods. "Yes, tomorrow is the final day of this week's class and tomorrow is feast day." You can feel the tension as the deadline looms.

Blueberry patch at Covert Farms

The Young Farmers Camp is but one of many things going on at Covert Farms. The third generation of the Covert family now running the farm is committed to connecting with the community

Tomato rows at Covert Farms

in a myriad of ways. Early September is the Festival of the Tomato. Outstanding in the Field is their ultra-gourmet farm dining experience, with visiting chefs, local wines, and fresh produce from the farm. Each weekend there are farm tours, conducted in a flaming-red vintage truck.

But it's not necessary to wait for a tour or a festival to sample the organic vegetables of Covert Farms. Lunch is served every day on a covered patio or out on the grass, and the menu changes according to what's fresh that day (or hour). It might be a purslane salad topped with local goat cheese, walnuts, dried cherries from the farm, and a tangy, lemony dressing. Dessert could be a popsicle made from last year's luscious frozen fruit. The plates and flatware are mismatched and the ambience is slightly chaotic, but the food is bursting with flavour and it's impossible to find anything fresher.

In addition to its own vegetables, the market showcases tangy vinegars and ripe cheeses, as well as plump heads of garlic from the Grown with Love Garlic Farm down at the bottom of the hill. To top off the experience, there is a u-pick flower garden next to the patio. Covert Farms has a good vibe. The owners and staff are proud of their products and excited to share information about organic farming. That enthusiasm is infectious.

Paradise (photo courtesy of the McDonald collection)

Covert Farms
38614 107th Street
Oliver, BC

A hike up the bluffs followed by lunch or a wine tasting at Covert Farms is an all-day affair. If you're thinking of picking berries too, I would suggest returning another day, preferably in the morning in order to avoid the heat.

Vineyard on the Naramata Bench overlooking Okanagan Lake

6. A Year in the Life of a Vineyard

All this talk about wine, but what about the vineyard? Winemakers go on and on about how the wine is made in the vineyard, but let's face it: it's the wine that gets all the glory. However, it's in the vineyard that the stakes are highest, where it feels like a gamble every year. Will the buds break on time? Will summer be warm enough for ripening? Will the autumn chill come too soon? Will there be a killing frost?

The vineyard's year begins in January, when it is a somewhat bedraggled-looking place, with straggly branches left over from last year's crop, a few forgotten bunches still clinging to the vines, and precarious mantles of snow perched on the trellis wires. Snow and mud lie everywhere. All of this under a leaden grey sky. But it's an important time for the vineyard because it's pruning season. The pruned canes are left on the ground, to be chopped up by a flail mower, a process that puts compost and nutrients back into the soil. The vineyard looks a lot neater after that, although a little scalped.

By March, it's time to tie down the remaining canes. With a little luck, buds are now starting to show the first signs of life. Tiny pointed protuberances form on the vines, giving a sense of hope that the season has begun. Then the agonizing wait for bud break—that crucial phase when the buds push through their silvery, velvety capsules to form miniature, delicate, green leaf clusters. It's unlikely that this magical moment will happen before April—even May in some locations. But everyone starts waiting for it in March!

As spring progresses and temperatures rise, those miniature individual leaves grow into larger leaves and then into shoots, which will eventually need to be inserted into the trellis wires in order to keep them from flopping all over the place. This process is called tucking but could as easily be referred to as neatening, since that's the overall effect. The newly tucked shoots are now more able to grow up, rather than out. Errant shoots poking up from the base of the vines and out along the trunks, disrespectfully called suckers, are completely useless. These poor things are

(top and bottom) Vineyards in various seasons

ruthlessly plucked away to give every opportunity to the productive shoots above.

Now the next miracle occurs—the flowering stage, when pale, self-pollinating, aromatic little flowers begin to emerge. Shortly after the flowering stage, real clusters of tiny grapes begin to form. Hard as rocks and green as peas, they are the beginning of what will be this year's harvest.

High summer is a wild time in the vineyard because this is when the vines go crazy. The shoots grow so quickly that it's almost impossible to keep them under some kind of control. More tucking, farther and farther up the trellis wires, as the vines

grow faster and faster and the leaves grow as big as dinner plates at a Chinese buffet. In addition to being tucked, lateral shoots have to be thinned in order to allow decent air flow through the canopy. The longest shoots are hedged (lopped off) when they burst over their boundaries at the tops of the trellis wires. The vineyard looks its lushest at this point in the year, with magnificent foliage

Van Westen Vineyards just before harvest

and vines growing in every direction, all in one chaotic scene.

But while those vines are running wild, the grapes are slowly ripening, and by August they begin to change colour. This is called *veraison*. In order to give maximum sunlight to those precious clumps of grapes, now turning a glorious rosy hue, some of the leaves need to be plucked down at the cluster level. But it's not only the leaves that have to be thinned. Hundreds of clusters are also chopped off, to ensure that the remaining clusters ripen and are of the highest quality. To protect those sweetening grapes from marauding flocks of starlings, a system of netting is placed over the rows of vines. Now begins the season when nervous vineyard owners and impatient winemakers are most often seen pacing up and down the rows, tasting, tasting, tasting.

As the grapes finish ripening, the leaves begin to turn, some to a tawny gold and others to a fiery red. Depending on the varietal and the location, the harvesting process can begin as early as September, but it is more likely an October event. The later the harvest, the scarier it is: a killer frost could finish off the leaves, and since ripening of the grapes depends on photosynthesis, this would be a disaster. But at some point, again with a little luck, the testing is done, the grapes are sweet enough, and the acid levels are low enough. It's

Artemisia Vineyard (photo courtesy of John Niddrie)

time to harvest! The bins arrive and the picking crew assembles early on a frosty morning to begin the harvest. It doesn't matter how often this ritual is repeated, it's always an exciting time. Clip, thunk, clip, thunk. The pails fill quickly with heavy clumps of sweet, deep purple grapes. Carry the pails to the bins. Load the bins on the tractor. Away they go—to the winery, where the winemaker is waiting.

It doesn't take long to harvest grapes, considering how long it takes to grow and ripen them! A few hours and it's done. After a quick celebratory gathering, a cup of hot coffee and a piece of cake, everyone leaves. The vineyard is suddenly quiet. The remaining leaves continue turning colour with the freezing temperatures of late autumn and eventually fall off the vines. Now the vineyard is alone—until January, when it begins all over again.

Vaseux Lake, with McIntyre Bluff in the distance

7. Corkscrew Drive

There were rumours of a couple of wines—not so well known, real sleepers—available south of Okanagan Falls, a town best known for Tickleberry's ice cream. One of the wines was a mysterious Merlot, the other a rare Riesling. Where? I asked. Corkscrew Drive was the answer.

Corkscrew Drive is one of those semi-back roads of the Okanagan that are nice to drive, but a dream to cycle. Quiet, hardly any traffic, stunning views around every turn, vineyards and farms and foliage to inspect—it definitely works better on a bike. This isn't so much "lake" country as it is "mountain" country, for the dominating feature of Corkscrew Drive is McIntyre Bluff.

Along the way are a few wineries, including Stag's Hollow.

Modest in comparison to some of the architectural showcases of the Okanagan Valley, it has no celebrity-chef restaurant, no soaring tower from which to observe the winemaking process, no performance space for visiting musicians. Simply a small tasting room and very good wine,

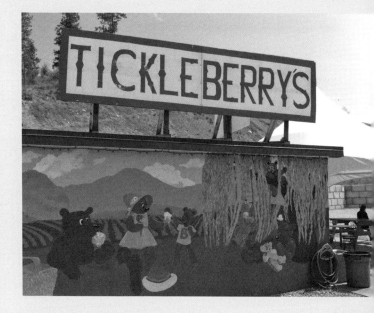

particularly their Merlot. Merlot sometimes gets a bad rap—it's sort of the Chevrolet of wine. Not like those Porsche Pinot Noirs or Cadillac Syrahs. Stag's Hollow Winery's Renaissance Merlot is divine—mocha and cherry and coffee flavours, and oh so polished. I love to have a few bottles on hand in my cellar. Winemaker Dwight Sick credits

45

Wild Goose Vineyards

some of the smoothness to the tightly grained Spanish barrels that he uses to age the wine.

A short pedal north from Stag's Hollow is Wild Goose Vineyards.

One of British Columbia's first farm-gate wineries, it obtained its licence in 1990, shortly after Lang Vineyards, farther up the valley on the Naramata Bench, obtained theirs. Two generations of the Kruger family own Wild Goose Vineyards. Adolf "Fritz" Kruger, the father, had been a devoted amateur winemaker for years back in Vancouver, and this passion for wine eventually motivated him to invest in some land in the Okanagan Valley in 1984. For the first few years he and his sons, Hagen and Roland, grew grapes for other wineries. But over time it became clear that what they really wanted to do was make their own wine.

They were some of the first vintners in the valley to plant northern European grape varieties, such as Gewürztraminer and Riesling. And although Wild Goose produces a wide selection of wines, several of which have won prestigious prizes, including seven Lieutenant Governor's Awards for Excellence, a record for a small winery, my taste buds tell me that their Riesling is extra special. The first impression is a little fruity, with hints of peach and apple, but at the end you're left with an amazing clean crispness. As Roland says, "People don't remember the architecture—they remember the quality of the wine and the people who sold them the wine." And in this case, the people who sell the wine are also the people who make the wine. This is a place where you can jump on your bike, cruise winding and scenic Sun Valley Way out of Okanagan Falls, and show up at Wild Goose in time to unpack a picnic lunch on their patio, then wash it down with you know what—a chilled glass of that award-winning Riesling.

Stag's Hollow Winery
2237 Sun Valley Way
Okanagan Falls, BC

Wild Goose Vineyards
2145 Sun Valley Way
Okanagan Falls, BC

Vaseux Lake

8. Vaseux Lake: A Birder's Paradise

We drifted about in the sweltering, sheltered lagoon—two canoes, three people—gazing at a flotilla of Canada geese sailing by. Two painted turtles slithered off their log. Then, out of the corner of my eye, I saw them. Three fully decked-out and completely loaded voyageur canoes drifting through the narrow lagoon entrance, flags flapping in the breeze. What?! When the participants stopped paddling and these impressive vessels glided to a stop, we sidled over, curious and amazed. "Who are you guys? Where did you get those canoes?" They laughed at our astonishment and explained that they were part of a guided birding expedition, one of dozens of events at the Meadowlark Nature Festival. Our curiosity sated, we settled in for an hour of concentrated birding, eavesdropping as best we could on the professional bird expert leading the Vaseux Lake expedition.

⌇⌇⌇

Vaseux seems fairly nondescript when compared to its swanky neighbours, Skaha and Osoyoos Lakes. No curving sandy beaches. No upscale condo developments. But Vaseux is special for one reason: birds! It even has a special designation—Important Bird Area (IBA). The marsh at the north end of Vaseux Lake is one of the last remaining Okanagan wetlands, and the meandering Okanagan River that feeds into the marsh is part of the only 2.7 kilometres of river that hasn't been diked into submission. The lake can be experienced from a few different angles, none of which include motors. For that reason alone, it qualifies as a "slow" experience.

The first and most accessible way to experience Vaseux is from Highway 97. Directly opposite a set of imposing cliffs is a turnoff to the Vaseux Lake viewing platform. A series of raised boardwalks leads through the marshy area to a final raised viewing structure. Along the way, strategically placed benches invite you to sit and watch and listen. Even though this pathway is close to the highway, it is strangely quiet, except for the birds, of course.

My husband, Alan, is an avid birder, which afforded me the luxury of simply strolling along behind him on the boardwalk while he tossed out his observations: song sparrow, yellow warbler, marsh wren. He wasn't actually seeing them; he was identifying them by their songs. When we sat down to do some serious birding, we began to see—not just hear—some action as the birds darted in and out of the birch foliage and glided around the cattails. An enormous osprey hovered nearby, waiting for some unsuspecting fish to appear. It was all quite dramatic.

A second and equally effective way to see Vaseux Lake is by bike. No, not a special flotation bike, but rather one that can navigate a flat and relatively smooth section of the old Kettle Valley Railway line on the west side of the valley. In fact, our experience on this trail was, hands down, the best birding in the Vaseux Lake region. We started at the quaint little beach in downtown Kaleden, a few kilometres north of Okanagan Falls. Following the KVR signs, we pedalled along scenic Skaha Lake, with exposed geological wonders on our right, red-winged blackbirds and Lewis's woodpeckers (among many species) on our left. At Okanagan Falls, we had to abandon the natural world briefly, crossing Highway 97 and riding up Green Lake Road, but only until we reached Okanagan Falls Campground, where we cycled to the far end and soon caught the old KVR line again.

Now the fun began. In a couple of hours of pedalling through a wide variety of landscapes—open ponderosa pine grasslands, cattail swamps, reedy ponds, leafy and shady enclaves, the shore of Vaseux Lake itself—we saw seventeen species of birds. Spectacular Bullock's orioles showing off in the sunlight. A great bald eagle, perched in a ponderosa pine, surveying its domain. An irritated osprey being harassed by a cheeky little red-winged blackbird. A marsh wren busily lining its nest with cattail fluff. A white-fronted goose pretending to be part of a small flock of Canada geese—unsuccessfully, it looked to me, for they simply pulled away from the poor guy. And the best—a life list species for Alan and, by default, for me: a yellow-breasted chat. It's not every day that Alan gets a life lister. He's seen almost everything it seems. But the day we biked the KVR along the western shore of Vaseux Lake, he really scored.

The third—and best, in my opinion—way to see the lake is to actually be *on* it. In a canoe or kayak.

You can launch a canoe from a number of places off Highway 97, and then it's pure pleasure, gliding along the quiet surface of the lake, ducking in behind a small island, poking around in hidden bays, or heading up to the northern end of the lake where it morphs into a marsh. Two protected lagoons at the south end of the lake are so quiet that they feel much wilder and farther from civilization

Voyageur canoes on Vaseux Lake (photo courtesy of the McDonald collection)

than they really are. In but a couple of hours of quiet observation, we saw Bullock's orioles, western kingbirds, violet-green swallows, song sparrows, ospreys (with fish in their talons), yellow warblers, mallard ducks, Canada geese, painted turtles, and a muskrat lodge. And the best treat of all was a solitary red-necked grebe, patrolling back and forth in front of our canoe. Upon closer inspection of the nearby shoreline, we discovered the reason for this supervision: a nest. This beautiful and almost primeval bird seems to best represent wild places—nature unchanged, a hope for the future.

Then the voyageur canoes reappeared, having fought their way up the swift-flowing waters of the Okanagan River. For a moment I was envious as I ogled their colourful and stately boats from our battered and trip-hardened aluminum craft. But you don't need a voyageur canoe to while away a day here—just a small boat, a picnic lunch, and plenty of sunscreen. Oh, and a pair of binoculars and a bird book would also be helpful, unless you have a resident expert on board.

Vaseux Lake is on Highway 97, 14.5 km north of Oliver and 10 km south of Okanagan Falls. Paddling on the lake is a nice half-day outing, as is cycling along the far side of the lake.

Mahoney Lake trail

9. Mahoney Lake Circuit

How many flowers can one slope support? That was my first thought when I saw the sea of gold that greeted us as we rounded a corner on the Mahoney Lake circuit trail. Thousands and thousands of balsamroot flowers were tilted at a jaunty angle to greet the warmth of the sun. The photo session began: stand at the bottom of the slope, gazing up at the display; sit in the midst of the happy blooms; try to find the very best clump of flowers. The afternoon soon turned into a gluttony of flowergazing.

But this area has a lot more to offer than flowers. Part of the White Lake Grasslands Protected Area, the Mahoney Lake trail is as beautiful to hike as it is fun to mountain bike. The mix of dry grasslands, open ponderosa pine forest, alkali ponds, and gneiss cliffs provides important habitat for a number of rare birds and animals. Although only eighteen metres deep, Mahoney Lake is a rare example of a meromictic lake, which means the various layers of water within the lake remain unmixed, resulting in incredible variations in temperature and salinity.

Ornithologist, prolific author, and special Okanagan consultant for the film *The Big Year*, Dick Cannings describes the White Lake area as one of his favourites for birding: "The wide open spaces, the fragrant smell of sage, the quiet."[1]

Balsamorhiza sagittata (arrowleaf balsamroot)

Although it's famous for rare birds like sage thrashers and white-headed woodpeckers, you will more likely be rewarded with the common yet equally beautiful bluebirds, hawks, and meadowlarks.

One slightly damp April morning, my husband and I saw thirteen different species. We didn't score the elusive sage thrasher, but we were surrounded by vesper sparrows darting among the twisted, gnarly sage bushes. Hawks stared down from their airy telephone pole perches, occasionally soaring to even greater heights before diving like bombers, intent on nabbing some innocent mouse. The brilliant yellow breasts of thousands of western meadowlarks flashed among the bushes. But it was their songs, not their breasts, that stole the show. Everywhere we wandered we were overwhelmed with the melodious meadowlark serenade. We also witnessed western bluebirds, with their intensely blue backs and contrasting rust-coloured breasts. And even better, the softer, almost painfully beautiful iridescent blue of the mountain bluebirds.

The White Lake Basin resembles the caldera of a huge extinct volcano. In fact, the basin is surrounded by curiously shaped volcanic cliffs, at the bases of which are some of the stateliest Douglas fir giants I've seen in the Okanagan Valley. California bighorn sheep graze here in the winter, and mule deer and bears frequent the area.

At the edge of the White Lake Basin protected area is the Dominion Radio Astrophysical Observatory, the only one of its kind in Canada. Its futuristic dishes and antennas add a touch of sci-fi mystery to the scene and hint at the important work being done by the astronomers and physicists huddled inside. The observatory is situated here because the surrounding hills screen out much of the radio interference caused by people and their toys. One radio telescope is so powerful—and so sensitive—that it could allegedly pick up a cell-phone signal from Mars! Adding a note of reality to the futuristic site is an enormous osprey nest perched on top of a scientific installation. When I was there, several tiny, inquisitive bald heads bobbed up and down in rhythmic succession as mamma brought goodies.

If your objective is to do the Mahoney Lake circuit, either on a bike or on foot, there are a couple of ways to begin. The first is at the White Lake trailhead on the Nature Trust property south of the lake. Just off Fairview-White Lake Road, you will find a gravel pull-off with a small parking lot and an information stand. My preference, however, is to start the trip from the opposite side, on Green Lake Road, for a number of reasons. The first is that the trail seems to flow more easily in that direction when you're riding a bike. The entire circuit takes about three leisurely hours

White-headed
woodpecker

Mountain bluebird

to ride, and that's including some birdwatching, flower sniffing, and a picnic along the way. Hikers have another good reason to start the trip here. For a more scenic option, they can begin from Green Lake Road on the regular trail, then watch for a sharp right turn up the ridge of Mount Keogan. The trail is quite faint as it goes uphill, but if you follow your instincts and stick close to the ridge, you will reach the top of this small mountain, where you can enjoy some classic Okanagan views of the surrounding hills and open forest. The third reason has nothing to do with hiking or biking, but with eating and drinking on the way home.

Partway down Green Lake Road, before dropping down the switchbacks into the main Okanagan Valley at the northern edge of Okanagan Falls, you will find the See Ya Later Ranch. A misnomer, since it's actually a winery. But it was begun as a working ranch in the early 1900s by the Hawthorne brothers. They and their families stayed on the ranch until shortly before it was sold to Major Hugh Fraser. Born in 1885, Fraser had a proper, if stuffy, upbringing in Eastern Canada, followed, somewhat ironically, by a stint in prison during the First World War. He lived on the ranch for more than forty-five years and, in the process, became something of a local celebrity. The folklore surrounding him is a bit murky, but the stories that have endured reveal him to have been an eccentric party host who was particularly fond of dogs. His hounds were given free run of the ranch and were ultimately laid to rest in a doggy cemetery

See Ya Later Ranch

that still exists at the winery. Fraser died in 1970 at the age of eighty-five. See Ya Later's wine label features a white dog decked out with angel wings in celebration of "man's best friend," the major's individualistic lifestyle, and the pioneering spirit that has always radiated from the winery site. In its own lighthearted way, the label respects the winery's colourful history.

See Ya Later's tasting room is a meticulously restored heritage stone home that dates back to the early 1900s. The view from the patio restaurant is spectacular! Looking out over the more than one hundred acres of land that make up Hawthorne Mountain Vineyard (all a part of the See Ya Later enterprise)—at first gentle slopes, then a plunge to the valley below—this truly is a room with a view.

See Ya Later makes lots of good wines, and reasonably priced ones too, but my favourite is their Gewürztraminer. Perhaps because this aromatic varietal thrives in the slightly cooler climate of the higher elevation, it seems the most appropriate wine for this winery. They must agree, since Hawthorne Mountain Vineyard has the largest planting of Gewürztraminer in North America, with sixty-five acres. I can't think of a better way to wrap up a good day of hiking or cycling on the Mahoney Lake circuit than to stop in at See Ya Later for a cool, spicy glass of Gewürztraminer.

Turn west off Highway 97 onto Highway 3, left on Twin Lakes Road, then left again onto White Lake Road. Now you are in the White Lake Basin. To reach the Mahoney Lake trailhead from the north side, turn right onto Fairview-White Lake Road. Stay on this road for 1 km, until you arrive at the trailhead, located next to a small information stand. To reach the Mahoney Lake trailhead from the other side, turn west off of Highway 97 at the north end of the town of Okanagan Falls onto Green Lake Road and head up the hill, past See Ya Later Ranch, for about 2 more km. You'll see a widening of the road immediately across from a yellow gate; park here. The trail starts at the gate. Cycling this loop takes a couple of hours. Hiking it is probably a three- to four-hour affair. Combined with the observatory or a glass of something at See Ya Later, the circuit is an ideal all-day outing.

Dominion Radio Astrophysical Observatory
717 White Lake Road
Penticton, BC

See Ya Later Ranch
2575 Green Lake Road
Okanagan Falls, BC

Linden Gardens

10. Kaleden's Linden Gardens

Some days are meant to be more civilized than others. Maybe dress up a little and set aside a few hours to enjoy some of the finer things in life. Flowers. Meandering pathways. Alfresco dining. More flowers. Linden Gardens, tucked away in the tiny village of Kaleden, is the place to be on one of those civilized days.

What began as a family tragedy has been converted into a living memorial and a sensory treat. When orchard workers Ken and Margaret Hayter lost their only son, they knew they would need to change their life in some dramatic way. They bought a seventy-five-year-old fruit farm on Linden Avenue and began to transform it. At first it was a hobby—something to occupy their minds and hands amid their grief. By 2006, they had reshaped the fruit farm into a nine-acre paradise of flowers, trees, shrubs, ponds, and streams.

The lushness of Linden Gardens is astonishing, particularly in contrast to the dry Okanagan hills that tower above Kaleden. As soon as you enter the garden, the temperature moderates, the humidity rises, the many hues of green overwhelm—and then there are the flowers. Acres of nodding white daisies, stately purple irises, passionate pink peonies, bold lilies, impossibly white dogwood trees, fragrant roses, elegant columbines, and ruby-red poppies. A veritable kaleidoscope of colour and scent caresses you.

Pathways lead everywhere. And every now and then, they lead nowhere. Which works just fine. Being deposited in the middle of a brilliantly green patch of grass ringed by tiger lilies and yellow irises with no apparent escape is not a serious problem. Through the trees you might spy a charming little bridge spanning a bubbling brook. Surely that must be the way? Getting lost is half the fun in this place. Stuffing your nose into a monstrous bloom is a fantastic way to initiate a sneezing frenzy. Missing the bridge is a surefire way of getting wet feet. But who cares? The sheer beauty of these gardens is a treat.

And then you begin to imagine the effort involved in creating this place. The trees are tall

Rudbeckia hirta
(black-eyed Susan)

and healthy. The grassy bits are scrupulously even. And the flower beds go on and on and on. Acres of colour. Acres of aroma. Acres of love went into these gardens.

When the nose and eyes and feet can take no more, there is relief at the end of the trail. Frog City Café is part of the experience, and what better way to satisfy a flower-honed appetite than to sit in the alfresco dining area under the shade of a sun umbrella, still within touching distance of the

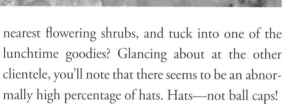

Papaveroideae (poppy)

Frog City Café at Linden Gardens

nearest flowering shrubs, and tuck into one of the lunchtime goodies? Glancing about at the other clientele, you'll note that there seems to be an abnormally high percentage of hats. Hats—not ball caps!

The chili-rubbed prawn wrap has a tiny zip to it, and the prawns are thick and juicy. Frog City's borscht is a refined version of this hearty beet soup, and it's laced with rich cream. The lily pad salad not only looks beautiful but is a creative mix of cool, crunchy, tangy, and—always—fresh. And finally, to try to extend this culinary experience a little bit longer—white chocolate lime cheesecake, with a strong cup of coffee.

Now that is a balanced combination of (mild) exercise, sensory stimulation, education (flower identification), and culinary delight. In a word—civilized.

Linden Gardens and Frog City Café
351 Linden Avenue
Kaleden, BC
Exploring the gardens takes a couple of leisurely hours. Combined with lunch, Linden Gardens makes a relaxing half-day outing.

On the trail to the Skaha Bluffs
(photo courtesy of the McDonald collection)

11. Rock Climbing at the Skaha Bluffs

From 1995 till 2006 the same scenario would play itself out in our house in Banff. As the work week wound down, my husband and I would begin checking the weather forecast, planning that weekend's adventure. It usually involved climbing. The excitement would grow. The packs would get packed. Then Friday morning would dawn, damp and dreary. We would look at each other, share a knowing nod, and throw the packs into the back of the car, confident that by 4:30 PM we would be on the road, headed for the Skaha Bluffs in the southern Okanagan Valley.

We would skid into the campground late that night, exhausted from the drive and the traffic but keen to hit the trail first thing in the morning, before the temperatures rose too high. The problem in those early years was the staircase. Everyone who climbed at Skaha dreaded it: a series of steep, widely spaced, and horrendously sun-exposed stairs leading from the parking lot up to the crags. That minor irritant faded into history when the area became a provincial park,

thanks to a lot of private money, some understanding landowners, and the political (and economic) will of the City of Penticton. It turned out that climbers, when there were enough of them, actually made a difference to the economy. Even climbers need to eat. And everyone knows they like to drink. Particularly wine, of which there was an abundance.

———

It's hard to say enough good things about the Skaha Bluffs. Hundreds of climbing routes spread throughout a series of parallel canyons, many with glorious views of Skaha Lake. Well-built trails, a detailed and comprehensive guidebook, and perfect weather that keeps on giving. The rock is two-billion-year-old gneiss, among the oldest rock in British Columbia. For the most part, the rocks' coarse-grained texture and the abundance of horizontal ledges on near-vertical faces make the bluffs a fingery vertical playground. But it's not all about the fingers. Some cliffs show a completely different

Fern Gully at the Skaha Bluffs (photo courtesy of the McDonald collection)

character, with steep overhanging walls studded with monster holds and splitter cracks.

The bluffs were first explored in the late 1960s by the University of British Columbia's Varsity Outdoors Club, but their ventures were tentative at best. In fact, it was almost by accident that the Skaha Bluffs became the climbing mecca they are

today. Howie Richardson, a biologist who moved to Keremeos in 1972, along with another local, Bob Cuthbert, noticed the glint of late-afternoon sunshine on what would later be known as the Great White Wall. They hiked in to take a look and were amazed at the climbing possibilities in front of them. When they turned around to hike out of the canyon, they almost fainted. Facing them was an entire *series* of walls: Doctors Wall, Red Tail, Fortress East Face. Endless potential on pristine walls that were completely hidden from view of the roadways below.

But the bluffs aren't only about climbing, although that is still the activity that lures most people into the canyons. Birdwatchers, hikers, trail runners, and naturalists are all drawn to this idyllic landscape. After the big fire of 1994, vegetation exploded at the bluffs. Aspen and birch trees, mock orange and saskatoon berry bushes. Desert wildflowers on the grassy slopes, and shy, elusive beauties in the shady glades. Several kinds of snakes frequent the crags, including the one that everyone talks—and worries—about, the western rattlesnake. The place is alive with birds, some quite rare. Of the approximately fifty pairs of canyon wrens in BC, at least six nest at the bluffs. Of the two hundred pairs of white-throated swifts, twenty-five live at the bluffs. California bighorn sheep, black bears, and moose. They're all here.

In those early days, when we used to make the pilgrimage to Skaha four or five times a year, the place was pretty quiet. It felt like a private climbing area, our little secret. But the secret's out. Now it's not unusual for a couple thousand people to visit the bluffs on a sunny spring weekend. The air is full of French and German, Polish, Spanish, and Japanese. The vehicles in the parking lot sport licence plates from around North America. Sometimes you even have to line up for popular routes.

We're cagey about going to the bluffs on weekends now. But thankfully, mid-week climbing is still a solitary activity. There might be a few other climbers in the canyons or, just as likely, a bird-watcher or two searching for some rare species. A trail runner training for the August triathlon race could easily float by. Or a couple of friends might be hiking, with picnic basket and hiking poles, tap-tapping their way along the rocky trails. On quiet autumn days, with the swifts swooping overhead and the carabiners clinking on our harnesses, I look up past the soaring ponderosas and the golden flutter of aspen leaves, beyond the ancient walls to the deep blue sky, and marvel at this vertical paradise called the Skaha Bluffs.

—∞—

Hikers and climbers aren't the only ones inspired by these rock formations. Engineer turned winemaker

Crags in autumn (photo courtesy of the McDonald collection)

Paul Gardner arrived in the area in 1996, opened Pentâge Winery just below the Skaha Bluffs, and couldn't stop gazing at one particular rock configuration on his land. Could there be a cave lurking underneath all that soil? A few years later Paul made the first backhoe cut and saw that there was indeed a continuation of a cave-like gap in between two walls of ancient, solid gneiss. And so the project of creating a natural cellar began: blasting, excavating, designing plans, getting permits, servicing the site with sewerage and natural gas and underground power.

Designing and building the forms for the first concrete pour took one full year. The main floor slab (which is two hundred and fifty-four cubic

Looking good! (photo courtesy of the McDonald collection)

metres) was poured in 2006. Several more slabs, combined with a layer of ridged foam to stop condensation in cold weather, steel reinforcements, piping for electrical services and carbon dioxide removal, stairs, massive glass doors, soaring skylights, and an elevated crush pad, and the building was finished in 2010. Although this particular cave took ten years to create and cost three times the projected budget, it is magnificent—and filled with wine, not surprisingly.

Visiting it, and tasting Pentâge's award-winning wines, is the perfect way to end a day at the Skaha Bluffs.

(top and bottom) Cave excavation at Pentâge Winery in progress . . . (photos courtesy of Pentâge Winery)

To reach Skaha Bluffs Provincial Park, travel 2.7 km south from Penticton on Lakeside Road, then turn east on Smythe Road. The Skaha Bluffs parking lot is at the end of Smythe Road. Whether you are hiking, biking, or climbing in this area, plan to spend an entire day. Or a week. Or more. It's heaven!

Pentâge Winery
4400 Lakeside Road
Penticton, BC

. . . and the result.

Aquilegia (columbine or granny's bonnet)
(photo courtesy of the McDonald collection)

12. Mount Brent: An Alpine Mecca

Occasionally I hear moaning and groaning about how sad it is that the Okanagan Valley has no alpine terrain—that special place where alpine fir and spruce trees are common, where open meadows are stuffed with a profusion of flowers, almost crass in their juxtaposition of bright colours. Those moaners haven't been to Mount Brent.

Four kilometres up Apex Mountain Road, toward the ski hill, a small dirt road leads off to the north. This old Shatford Creek logging road has been "decommissioned" but not very effectively. A further eight kilometres up that road (pretending not to be a road) is a trailhead with a modest little sign indicating the trail to Mount Brent. There are actually two trails, and, although they take completely different routes, both are rewarding. Particularly if you're there for the flowers.

Late July is probably the best time for these alpine beauties, but the worst for bugs. August is a little more reasonable in terms of the bugs, but the flowers aren't quite as crazily lush. Either way, it's worth the trek. The meadows are so luxuriant your shoes will squeak, and the Indian paintbrushes and marigolds, and fields of limpid blue lupine, are a veritable feast for the eyes.

Then, just as the terrain is becoming somewhat rougher and rockier, the summit! Yes, a real summit, with a real view, down into the Okanagan Valley, which appears from this vantage point like the deep trough it is. You can also see the Coast Mountain range to the west and the United States to the south. In the north, the vast high plateaus stretch out before you. Twelve kilometres return and an elevation difference of four hundred and forty-four metres make this a good half-day hike or, even better, an all-day affair with a mountaintop picnic thrown in.

Mount Brent—a taste of the alpine in the middle of the desert.

***Lupinus* (lupine)**
(photo courtesy of the
McDonald collection)

To reach the Mount Brent trailhead, drive west from
Penticton on Green Mountain Road, which turns into
Apex Mountain Road. After 4.1 km on the Apex road,
turn right onto the Shatford logging road and continue
for 3.7 km. Turn left and continue for 3.9 km, at which
point there is a fork in road. Stay left, and after 700 m
you will arrive at a trailhead in an old logging landing.
The Mount Brent hike is a nice day hike. No point in
rushing through all those flowers.

Walla Foods

13. Artisanal Middle Eastern Breads and Beer

Walla Foods is special. I first became aware of this miracle bakery one evening when a friend brought over a massive loaf of their Jewish rye. I sliced into the thick, crispy crust to discover the most attractive, golden-hued, moist and tender bread. I snuck a small piece while preparing dinner. No butter—just a quick sample. Impossible! The flavour was intense. The texture flawless. The aroma intoxicating.

"Where on earth did this bread come from?" I asked guiltily, as crumbs fell down my chin.

"Walla's bakery—in the old cannery building. Don't you know it?"

"No, but I'm going to!"

A week later, after we had finally eaten our way through that gigantic loaf, I toddled into Walla Foods. In a tiny hole in the wall along the unpretentious old cannery corridor that houses a shoe repair shop, a canoe manufacturer, and a brewery, I found what I thought must be the place. Outside the shop stood a few metal shelving units, almost completely empty save for half a dozen focaccia buns. I stepped inside. Nobody home. More empty shelves. I coughed to attract the attention of anyone who might be out back. A serious-looking man strode in, hairnet covering his crew-cut, hands and apron covered in flour.

"Yes?"

"Um, hi. I was wondering if you had any of those big loaves of Jewish rye?"

"It's Tuesday. Jewish rye is on Friday. Can't you see the schedule?" He pointed out a small, typed weekly schedule indicating his bread production.

"Oh, I see. So you don't have any Jewish rye today?"

"No, it's Tuesday. Today is wholewheat cranberry walnut. But it's gone. Here, take some of these." He put two focaccia into a paper bag and prepared to go back to his kitchen.

"Oh, sure, that would be fine," I mumbled. "How much do I owe you?"

"Nothing. Enjoy. And come back on Friday."

I did as I was told. Except that I didn't get the focaccia home. At least not both of them. One was gone by the time I hit the edge of the city. Amazing flavour and the perfect amount of olive oil and fresh Mediterranean herbs on top. My mouth is watering just writing about it now.

Friday arrived and I trotted back into the bakery. This time a fellow was seated at a small table outside the bakery, playing chess with the baker, who, I had learned by then, had a name—Benjamin Manea.

"Hi, I'm back. I was wondering . . ."

"You want the rye. Good. Today is Friday. Here it is." He lifted an imposing loaf off the metal shelf and presented it to me, as if on a silver platter. "You must not put in plastic."

"Pardon me?"

"Do not put in plastic," he repeated.

"Oh, okay, but I don't think I can eat it all today."

"Of course not. You can place in paper or put face down on the counter. Or you can freeze half. But don't put in plastic."

"Okay, definitely. I won't put it in plastic."

It was only after a half-dozen visits that the plastic lecture finally ended. But I don't blame him for insisting on the special care and maintenance of the Jewish rye. This bread does not deserve to be touched by plastic. And neither do the others: puttanesca sourdough with kalamata olives, capers, olive oil, and olive pesto; wholewheat cranberry walnut bread; rustic beer buns made with spent barley from the Cannery brewery; and more.

After I had made a few more visits to the bakery, Benjamin described his journey to Penticton, which had not been a direct one. Born in Romania, he was raised in Israel and then immigrated to Toronto. Finally, he moved to the Okanagan Valley in 2005. We started talking about baking and the concept of "slow." It turns out that Benjamin's attitude toward Slow Food and the entire slow movement is synchronistic with the thesis of this book. He acknowledged that the official Slow Food movement began in Italy twenty years ago but insisted that in his small Romanian village of Fǎlticeni, it was already alive and well thirty years earlier. In fact, he was born and raised in such a culture.

Although it wasn't labelled slow or organic, everything was homegrown and homemade of natural ingredients. It smelled like it was supposed to and tasted even better. He learned from his mother, who had learned from her mother. They baked bread, made their own egg

, simmered borscht, and stuffed tomatoes, peppers, and vine leaves. Even at an early age, he understood the importance of cooking—and eating. Everything was cooked on a coal-fired stove, baked in a wood-fired oven, and created by hand. Benjamin's first kitchen job was to carry drinking water in buckets from a hand-cranked pump at the end of the street.

There is a noticeable Mediterranean approach to Benjamin's style. He explained that the Romanian culture has strong Italian and French influences in its spoken language and art, and that its food resembles the rustic cuisines of Tuscany and Provence. *Givechi* is ratatouille; *mămăligă* is polenta. To complicate things even further, the mighty Austro-Hungarian Empire also left its mark on Romanian cuisine, with goulash and Viennese schnitzel and paper-thin strudel.

As a child in Communist Romania, Benjamin was accustomed to seeing empty shelves in the state-owned stores. (That might explain his comfort level with his own shop's empty shelves.) Life was hard, but everyone relied on the thriving black market. Even though the secret police could make life miserable, the water was clear, the soil and air were clean, and the food was healthy.

Benjamin brought this set of values to the Okanagan Valley, with its abundance of fresh food and wine, and he remains inspired to share his grandmother's rustic, unpretentious recipes with his customers. Absolutely everything is made by hand. Every loaf of bread. Every soup stock. Every individual focaccia bun! His soups take three days to make. Same with the bread. This is slow. Very slow.

Breads from Walla Foods

As for his heavenly croissants, he credits a Parisian baker for the coaching. But the rolls were not an easy win. "Baking croissants is like doing the tango," Benjamin says. "Unless you spend hours and hours folding and turning the pastry, all your knowledge and desire won't deliver the perfect croissant, and you will be forever lost in the land of mediocrity, without redemption or parole."

To complement the fabulous baking there are a variety of dishes. A few tables out front and a cozy little dining room round out the experience at Walla's. Brioche French toast for breakfast, gourmet focaccia sandwiches for lunch, plus thick and creamy mushroom and vegetable soups, hummus,

Mouthwatering meringues

baba ghanoush, tabbouli, labneh, matbucha, baklava, and more. He even does takeout. At one point I realized that I could stop cooking. I could simply come to Walla's!

"Yes. I do takeout," he nodded—seriously.

"But don't put in plastic?" I asked.

Finally a smile from this taciturn genius of a baker. "That's right. No plastic."

———

There is one more stop you should make in the cannery building, and it has to do with beer. Cool, refreshing beer. Hard to beat on a hot Okanagan day, particularly if you've just pedalled into town after a long day on the Kettle Valley Railway or up on the Three Blind Mice trails.

The Cannery Brewing Company is Penticton's answer to a local, all-natural microbrewery. This craft brewery opened in 2000 and has been producing uniquely flavoured beers ever since. Brewmaster Terry Schoffer is the talent behind the beautifully balanced list, and the varieties on offer are impressive: Blackberry Porter, Squire Scotch Ale, India Pale Ale, Wildfire IPA (named in honour of the many firefighters who work hard to keep the valley safe). But probably the most popular is the Naramata Nut Brown Ale. This is a full-bodied brown ale, with a hint of hops, a smooth finish, and a lovely lingering aftertaste.

In a valley overwhelmed with wonderful wines, it's good to know that beer lovers won't go thirsty.

Walla Foods—Mediterranean and Middle Eastern Artisan Bakery and Cafe
114-1475 Fairview Road
Penticton, BC

Cannery Brewing Company
112-1475 Fairview Road
Penticton, BC

Cannery Brewing Company's refreshing Blackberry Porter

A lemon tart from Wouda's Bakery

14. Apple Plaza, La Cucina, and Buy the Sea

Halfway down the "strip" on Penticton's Main Street is a nondescript little mall that outperforms its appearance. Apple Plaza, also known as the Okanagan Market, is home to good meat and fine bread. All that's missing are fresh vegetables. Seriously serious about food, this little plaza is a lifeline for people who live in the area and for visitors passing through.

At the back of Apple Plaza is Wouda's Bakery. Since the 1800s, five generations of the Dutch Wouda family have baked breads and pastries, passing down age-old techniques from father to son while embracing the modern creativity of each new generation—and now a new country. They bake thirty kinds of European-style bread, everything from skinny French baguettes to plump pumpkin-seed loaves. Their buns are crusty on the outside, soft and mellow inside. When I asked Andy Wouda, the baker, what makes this bakery Dutch, he pointed to the cream puffs, the vanilla slices, and the fern tarts filled with almond butter and a dollop of jam.

"We like our cream," he said. "And mocha." He grinned, indicating the hazelnut cakes.

He singled out his wife Amie's cherry chocolate brownie as the ultimate combination of rich chocolate and even richer butter. Amazing stuff. But my personal weakness at Wouda's is a shameful inability to resist their tarte au citron, apparently one of their most popular items. Made from hand-squeezed lemon juice and surrounded by a rich buttery pastry, these darlings simply melt in the mouth. Somehow, the tartness of the lemon almost fools one into thinking it's not that rich. Almost.

～～～

Across the plaza's open lobby is another gem—Tony's Meats. Hailing from Portugal's Azores, owner Tony Craveiro is passionate about meat. He's been handling it since he was eleven years old, when he began working with his father. He came to the Okanagan Valley in 1985, originally settling in Naramata, where he spent many years working in the orchards. But meat was in his blood,

Tony Craveiro, owner of Tony's Meats

cheese, each rack of ribs that he marinates in his own secret sauce. His beef comes from Merritt, British Columbia, and various farms in Alberta. The rest of his meat comes from around British Columbia—his pork from the Lower Mainland, his sausages from Vernon, and his chickens from Vancouver. His shop is brimful of wonderful mustards and sauces and cheeses and smoked meats. But to fully appreciate Tony's Meats, it's best to do the obvious—eat some meat! The one item he cannot keep in stock is his Maui ribs. Ask him how he cuts them, how he marinates them, how to cook them. He loves every aspect of the process and is happy to share.

———

Farther down Main Street is La Cucina, a modest little European market and delicatessen well worth a visit. Another Portuguese import, Carlos Mendonça first brought his family to Kitimat in northern BC. When they moved south to Penticton in 1973, his father, Manuel, bought a little general store on this corner of Main Street and operated it as such for almost twenty years. Then Carlos got involved and developed it into a gourmet specialty store with a dizzying array of culinary products: Portuguese-style egg drops, German spaetzle, Italian pastas, delectable olive oils, specialty vinegars, pasta bowls, and cheese, cheese, cheese. The cheese display

and in 1998 he got a chance to return to his roots. Never imagining what a big, successful business it would become, he opened a small meat market. Then he worked and worked and worked—seven years straight at one point, without one day off.

Tony takes his business very seriously—and personally. He cares about each piece of beef that he trims of fat, each pork loin that he surrounds with bacon, each chicken breast that he stuffs with Swiss

is heartbreakingly beautiful—it features two hundred varieties. Much of it is from abroad, but the buffalo mozzarella comes from Ontario and Carlos thinks it's great. I agree. This is a place where you can find the ingredients that, when combined with some fresh veggies from the market, a glorious piece of fish, and a good loaf of bread, are all you need for a veritable feast.

⸻

Also on Main Street is Buy the Sea Seafoods, which the Stokes family opened in 1992. So successful is Buy the Sea that they now have a second store in West Kelowna. They explain that everything about fish is important: where it comes from, how fresh it is, how it's caught or raised. It is a pleasure to come in to Buy the Sea, to gaze at the gleaming, fresh fish and smell that special aroma. Salmon, tilapia, tuna, crab, or oysters—it's all good. The staff is knowledgeable about fish and seafood, and they make good suggestions about how to prepare what you buy and what to serve it with. As Samantha Stokes points out, "We love fish here."

You can even enjoy these fishy delights without ever leaving the building. My parents won't leave Penticton without stopping at Buy the Sea for fish and chips. The ambience is simple, but the fresh tuna is lightly battered and cooked to a crispy finish while the chips are bursting with real potato flavour. Yum.

More delights from Wouda's Bakery

Apple Plaza
1848 Main Street
Penticton, BC

La Cucina European Market
1204 Main Street
Penticton, BC

Buy the Sea Seafood
106-2100 Main Street
Penticton, BC

Burger 55

15. Eating Out in Penticton

It's impossible to tackle the restaurant scene in a place as food-oriented as the Okanagan Valley. It's not fair. In fact it's probably best to just wander around, ask questions, and then choose according to your palate and—obviously—your pocketbook.

But still, there are some unusual places that might go unnoticed and shouldn't. One such place is Wild Scallion, an affordable, healthy hole in the wall on Front Street. Its real claim to fame is takeout food. Five dollars a box. It's a kind of delightful marriage of fast food and slow food. Fantastic creations are pulled together by Chef Hong Lac for the dozens of clients who line up at the takeout window and for the few who fit inside at the half dozen tiny tables. The green lentil curry is my favourite.

Tucked away on a side street in downtown Penticton is an unusual place. The location isn't the most aesthetic setting for a restaurant, but Burger 55 owners Chris Boehm and Steve Jones couldn't care less. They make burgers. Probably the best burgers in town. And everyone knows it. The 1950s-style restaurant, which was inspired by a Vegas road trip, is thronged with locals and visitors sidling up to the bar, custom-designing juicy, flavourful burgers that they then whisk back to their offices or, better yet, consume directly outside the door. Oh, did I mention that Burger 55 is located in a parking lot? Maybe not so charming. But who cares when you are inhaling one of these beauties, along with some of their crispy fries? One side of the orange-and-white cube that serves as the restaurant is reserved for customers with dogs. The other side (next to the creek)—prime seating—is without dogs. And believe it or not, this place is licensed. Yes, you can order a beer or a glass of wine.

Farther up Main Street you'll find a Penticton institution—Theo's, built in 1976. Nikos Theodosakis categorizes his Greek offerings as Okanagan-Mediterranean cuisine. He and his mother, Mary, have discovered a number of the wild greens they used back in Crete here in the Okanagan Valley, including nettles. They source many of their fresh ingredients from Covert Farms' organic gardens.

In winter, a blazing fireplace warms the funky interior, with its traditional white walls and wooden floors. In summer, the shaded, leafy courtyard is the closest thing to Crete you'll find in North America. With dried herbs draped overhead it even smells like Crete—an Okanagan version of that arid island.

A few blocks away is The Bench Artisan Food Market. Rarely have I found a more enjoyable hangout than The Bench. Perched on Vancouver Hill, on the way out of Penticton heading to Naramata, The Bench is *the* place to be, for many reasons.

First off, it's a coffee shop.

But such yummy baking to go with that coffee! Their lemon scones will drive you to distraction—so light and fluffy and tart. It's hard to resist

Coffee break!

The Bench Market

Theo's Restaurant

stopping in for one, along with a steaming mug of strong coffee or subtle herbal tea. In fact, according to original co-owner Dawn Lennie, some people have given up resisting, for their most loyal customers pop in two or three times a day.

But a snack is only the preamble. It's perfectly acceptable to come for a mid-morning snack and then stay on for lunch. Maybe a change of table, moving outside onto the patio as the day warms up, but why not linger? The Bench specializes in deliciousness: everything from chicken salad panini (which seem to be their all-time favourite) to a salad trio (the customer gets to choose which three).

The Bench is that curious combination of urban chic and grassroots casual. It began as the brainwave of two sisters: Dawn Lennie and Debbie Halladay. One of their original mandates was to serve local, at all costs. And local they have remained. Whenever possible, head chef—and new owner—Stewart Glynes uses local cheeses, local breads, local meats, and local fruits and vegetables. The amazing productivity of this valley is evident in the restaurant's tasty meals and the seasonality of their menus.

And if for some reason you couldn't get to The Bench for a while, you wouldn't be completely out of luck because you could ask them to come to you. Yes, they cater! Or if time were a limiting factor, you could stop to pick something up from their grocery: local cheese from Poplar Grove Cheese, frozen Indian cuisine from Vij's Restaurant in Vancouver, specialty oils and vinegars, house-made dips, bamboo picnic dishes, pickles, biscotti, wine jelly, truffles, or cookbooks.

Even The Bench's walls, covered in artwork, connect to the community. The displays change twice a month and always feature a local artist. And on Sunday afternoons, it's not just the visual artists who enjoy profile: musicians perform out on the patio and the scene gets even better.

Wild Scallion
75 Front Street
Penticton, BC

Burger 55
85 Westminster Avenue East
Penticton, BC

Theo's Restaurant
687 Main Street
Penticton, BC

The Bench Artisan Food Market
368 Vancouver Avenue
Penticton, BC

(middle and bottom) The Bench selection

Bartlett Pear Still

16. Farmers' Markets

One of the greatest success stories emanating from the Slow Food movement in Western Canada is the explosion of farmers' markets. Some of the very best markets in the province are here in the Okanagan Valley. No surprise, since they subscribe to the principle of farm to table, and this valley is full of farms and orchards.

Penticton's market takes place each Saturday morning, and it's not unusual to see a mini traffic jam on Main Street as chefs and homemakers and visitors rush into town, grab their market shopping bags, top up their coffees at one of the many coffee shops, don sun hats, and head out! Several city blocks are closed off to vehicular traffic for the market as the walkers and vendors and street performers take over.

The vendors create a moveable and seasonal feast for the eyes and nose and palate. The first spring markets are tentative yet hopeful affairs, limited to early greens—bags of spicy arugula and tender young lettuce—and bright red radishes. As the season ramps up the choice of vegetables grows. Slender green beans in neat little bundles nestle up against bunches of sweet baby carrots. Bulging bags of Swiss chard and deep green spinach muscle out the baby beets. Bouquets of vivid, fresh-cut flowers at amazingly good prices. Eggs so fresh you already know the colour of the yolks. Blushing apricots and bursting cherries. Soft, ripe peaches and deep purple Italian prune plums. Golden honey flavoured with lavender or pear. Tiny jewel-toned

$3.99 / BASKET

Fresh, fresh, fresh!

(top and bottom) Fruit abundance at the farmers' market—shop to your heart's content

jars of raspberry and rhubarb jam. Hard cheese and soft cheese. Blue cheese and white cheese. Mild cheese and smelly cheese. Armloads of aromatic lavender. Crusty baguettes and dark, heavy loaves of artisanal bread. Pastries so buttery rich they're sinful to look at. As the season advances, the melons and squash and pumpkins and apples begin to take over. Mature carrots stacked next to mounds of turnips and beets. Tomatoes: yellow ones, green ones, and red ones. Designer tomatoes. Vine tomatoes. Sun-drenched, unbelievably juicy tomatoes that burst in your mouth.

⚬⚬⚬

Throughout the valley, from Osoyoos to Vernon, in the lakeside village of Peachland, the farming town of Armstrong, and even the big city of Kelowna, consumers have discovered the value and pleasure of buying locally produced food. Knowing where the food was grown, who grew it, how it was grown, when it was picked, what the chickens ate, how long the cheese was aged— these are the benefits of buying directly from the farmers and producers.

Not everyone has the space or time or inclination to grow a garden. I do, so I probably spend less time at farmers' markets than most. But even with a garden outside my door, I can't resist the temptation to indulge in that Saturday morning

Russian red garlic

ritual, wandering among the earth's bounty, meeting the people who grow and make the stuff, visiting with neighbours, sharing recipes, planning dinner parties, being part of the community that is "food." It's one of the best shows in town—any town, all the towns, up and down the valley.

It's hard to beat eating food this fresh, but sometimes it's good to think ahead. Canada's winters are long. As folksinger Jeremy Fisher reminds us, some of our grandmothers' summer kitchen traditions are worth embracing as our own:

Peaches on the shelf
Potatoes in the bin
Supper's ready, everybody come on in
Taste a little of the summer . . .
My grandma put it all in jars.[1]

The schedules for the Okanagan Valley farmers' markets are in Appendix C. You can plan an entire trip around them.

View over Okanagan Lake, Penticton, and Skaha Lake

17. Cycling the KVR and Three Blind Mice

The Kettle Valley Railway, known as the KVR, is an abandoned railway bed that winds its way through southern British Columbia between Midway and Hope. When the British Columbia government purchased the KVR corridor, it promised to preserve the railbed for future use. Because it's a typical railway bed, with track grades that never exceed 2.2 percent, the KVR is ideal for recreational cycling, walking, running, and horseback riding. It's over six hundred kilometres in length, and some of the most scenic sections are in the Okanagan Valley, including a stretch that heads north from Penticton along the east side of Okanagan Lake above Naramata Road.

A good place to start pedalling this section is partway up Vancouver Hill in northern Penticton. A well-marked trail meanders through a quiet residential area and along a series of spectacular clay hoodoo formations that plunge to the lake below. Frequent viewpoints invite you to stop and gaze back at the city, at the marina directly below, or at the picturesque sailboats whisking along the lake. After passing a cemetery, the trail rolls along through the historic King Family Vineyard, with luxurious grape-laden vines on either side. It crosses the impressively airy Randolph Creek trestle to emerge amid an ongoing feast for the eyes: apple orchards, cherry orchards, vineyards, and wineries. At the precise moment when the sun has become a tad oppressive and sweat is starting to run down your back, there it is—the Trail Store, right beside the KVR and offering cool drinks and ice cream!

⌘

The KVR crosses Naramata Road after a couple of kilometres and then climbs gently through more vineyards and along behind a number of Naramata Bench wineries, among them Hillside Winery. Hillside understands cyclists' needs, and they have thoughtfully placed a sign with their daily lunch menu at the top of a convenient little trail that drops down to the patio restaurant. There is no point in resisting because smell, like sound, travels

The Trail Store

this dark, breezy tunnel. At the other end, there is a dramatic shift in view, for this is where the lake makes a dogleg on its journey toward Kelowna.

The Naramata Bench section of the KVR is pretty domestic, some might even say "tamed," thanks to the agricultural nature of the Bench. But it's not all tame. There are wildflowers galore, flowering shrubs, chirping marmots, towering ponderosas, aromatic sage, and whispering grasses. And there are snakes. They seem to love to slither out onto the flat, dark surface of the trailbed and warm themselves. Completely harmless, assuming you don't run over them, they do add a little frisson to the experience.

If you turn around at the tunnel, it's all downhill back to Penticton. A gentle, steady, effortless glide. I can't think of a more beautiful bike ride.

———

up, and the aromas emanating from the Hillside Bistro are ridiculously seductive.

The route continues past more wineries, more trim, undulating vineyards, miniature horse pastures, and occasional benches for enjoying the increasingly beautiful view—on and on, all the way to the spectacular cliff-bordered tunnel. After an hour or more of pedalling steadily upwards, you'll discover a fantastic place to cool off, simply by wheeling into

Three Blind Mice is the strenuous alternative to the KVR and is becoming increasingly popular with mountain bikers. *Blind* is the right descriptor for this area because that's how I feel when I'm up there, trying to figure out where I've been and where I'm going. There is actually a map, available on the Sweet Singletrack website, and some people carry a GPS to find their way around. But the simplest and best navigational tool is Okanagan Lake. It's always to the west. And it's always down.

I did mention that Three Blind Mice is strenuous, didn't I? The most popular approach to this veritable maze of trails is from Riddle Road. Riddle Road, up to the entrance of Three Blind Mice, is the first hint of what's to come. It's up. Huffing past the Riddle Road Retreat Bed & Breakfast, then around a small curve, you arrive at the Pearly Gate. Ah, heaven must be near. It depends on your definition of heaven. If unlimited single-track trails and fabulous scenery are what you consider heaven, it's aptly named.

From the gate, you enter a kind of gully system where, in times gone by, a 5.6-kilometre chute transported logs from the upper slopes down to Okanagan Lake. In order to hasten their journey, the chute was lubricated with water and grease. Down below, between the logs and their final destination—the lake—was the very inconvenient Naramata Road. To prevent potential collisions, a bugler was stationed at the edge of the road and would warn drivers who might be in the wrong place at the wrong time.

Although there is no longer a log chute, the topography remains chute-like: steep, narrow, and directly down to the lake. The trail winds up through a field of poison ivy and then becomes steeper, before it veers left on a switchback, up onto a flat section of ponderosa forest. The wide track eventually narrows to a single track and then to intermittent rock steps.

Three Blind Mice: a biker's paradise!
(photo courtesy of the McDonald collection)

As you climb higher the views get better and the terrain becomes more technical.

Occasional old Mice signs appear, nailed to pine trees, but most of these have been replaced with signs indicating the many trails: Three Witches, Black Bear, White Tail, Narnia, Bobcat, Cougar, Fred. There are dozens and dozens of trails, almost seventy at last count.

One of the shorter loops, taking perhaps one to two hours, is the White Tail trail. This is the lowest route, leading up from the Pearly Gate along a series of terraces. Mostly in open grassland terrain,

View over Naramata and Okanagan Lake from the Kettle Valley Railway

Three Blind Mice trail (photo courtesy of the McDonald collection)

it occasionally dips through shady, leafy deciduous forests that swarm with warblers in the spring. It then drops down to Turnbull Creek, which is crossed on a wobbly, slanted bridge. This is known as First Crossing.

Farther along is the Drop Out Junction sign,

from where the most direct route along this elevated bench is to turn left, up a nasty series of rock steps (pushing the bike) and onto another level bench. Eventually, the trail meanders back down, popping out onto the KVR slightly north of the toilets.

The spring flowers on the Three Blind Mice trails are splendid, everything from grassland posies to creek-side beauties. The balsamroot season is spectacular—entire slopes are covered with nodding golden blossoms. At that time of year you can bike at any hour of the day, but later in the season, when temperatures rise and the grass crackles underfoot, midday is a time to avoid at all costs. Most of the cycling on Three Blind Mice is either up or down. Energy is required. Legs must be strong and water bottles must be full! Autumn brings a respite from the heat, and it's not uncommon to see riders up here on a cool winter's day.

One of the best things about Three Blind Mice is the variety of trails for all kinds of ability levels. Well—almost. There are no easy trails. But they are as pleasurable to hike or run as they are to bike. One advantage to hiking is that you notice a greater amount of detail, but unfortunately you miss the thrilling downhill runs. Hundreds of trails in an almost-wilderness set high above the agricultural Naramata Bench—a naturalist's or adrenalin-seeker's mecca.

View over Okanagan Lake in the fall

Road up to Munson
Mountain in the winter

18. Poplar Grove Wine and Cheese and Munson Mountain

It's always nice to work up an appetite for wine or cheese, or both. In the case of Poplar Grove wine and cheese, the handiest place to get that hit of exercise is on Munson Mountain. Penticton's signature mountain, this volcanic plug sits above Okanagan Lake, watching over the Penticton cemetery at its foot.

Although most of the required elevation can be gained by a narrow access road, there remains a short hike to reach the summit, where the panoramic views extend from the city of Penticton to the Naramata Bench and up the lake toward Summerland. You could spend a lot of time on that summit.

But not if you're hungry for cheese. For that, it's best to drop down the trail, jump onto a mountain bike, and head north on the Kettle Valley Railway, an easy ride through rolling vineyards. Cheese is not far away. Turn left down Poplar Grove Road to the *fromagerie* of the same name. This is the best place to taste—and buy—the wonderful Poplar Grove cheeses that have been a signature of this valley for years. At the fromagerie, set amid the mature vines of the Poplar Grove vineyard, Gitta Peterson has been handcrafting delectable rounds of cheesy heaven since 1990.

Each one of her four varieties has its charm. Naramata Bench Blue is a creamy, mild blue cheese that is brine salted, aged for three weeks, hand flipped each week, and then wrapped. There is a hint of sharpness in this cheese and a soft, mellow "finish." But for the ultimate decadent experience, you must try the sinfully rich, soft, white double-cream Camembert. Brine salted, then aged for three weeks, this soft cheese is hand flipped twice a week to ensure an even growth of its characteristic velvety white coat. It melts in the mouth. The Harvest Moon Washed Rind takes up to five weeks to mature, and the Tiger Blue, anywhere from seven to eight weeks to achieve its sharper taste.

I asked Gitta how she markets her products,

since I've seen them in stores across Western Canada.

"I don't," she said.

"You must," I countered.

"No, really, it's strange, but my distribution strategy is pretty simple—it's word of mouth."

What a success story. Thanks to the consistently high quality, she can barely keep up with the demand. Here in this modest out-of-the-way nook on the Naramata Bench, at the end of a lane called Poplar Grove, magic happens.

Poplar Grove Winery, on the other hand, is neither modest nor out of the way. It clings to the lower slopes of the south side of Munson Mountain, overlooking Penticton and Okanagan Lake. Spectacular during the day. Glamorous by night. This is an upscale experience. The building was designed to take full advantage of the site and has a minimalist feeling, both inside and out. Even the landscaping is carefully planned, with sage, lavender, and poplars framing the winery. The long, slender building includes a working winery, a showcase barrel room, and a generous tasting room—nothing kitschy here. Simple lines, expansive glass, killer views. Class. Class. Class. And so are the wines.

The Poplar Grove portfolio includes six core wines: Pinot Gris, Chardonnay, Cabernet Franc, Merlot, Syrah, and a blend called Legacy. Their reds are particularly memorable because after they have spent eighteen months in French oak barrels, the winery continues to age them for an additional eighteen to thirty months, maturing the wines in bottles. The extra time investment is obvious because these wines are ready to drink when they are released. They win all kinds of awards, which only adds to their reputation.

But for many, the pièce de résistance is the Vanilla Pod. What on earth is that? you might ask. Paul and Sheila Jones began the Vanilla Pod restaurant across the lake in Summerland. After gaining a loyal clientele and establishing an original tapas menu paired with an informed selection of Okanagan wines, they crossed the lake to join Poplar Grove. Executive Chef Bruno Terroso has created possibly the best dining experience in Penticton.

Whoa—that's saying a lot. But take a look. Inside, the space is small and cozy, with a blazing fireplace to warm winter diners and an unobstructed view of the kitchen, where the chef and his assistants bustle about. It's great to see what's happening in the kitchen. The large patio is the place to be in warmer seasons, protected from the sun by gleaming suspended sails. And then there is that view of the lake and city, which, as the evening wears on, comes alive with thousands of twinkling lights. Glam indeed.

But even if all of that were to disappear—poof—there would still be the food. And the Vanilla Pod does not fail. The tasting menu is irresistible, like tapas on steroids. The grilled eggplant topped with portobello mushrooms and goat cheese has a soft, mellow flavour that invites you to linger on each individual taste. Next is a crispy flatbread smothered in a creamy chicken creation that melts in the mouth. Grilled salmon basted with a balsamic vinaigrette sauce is sweet and succulent. Then, a sensibly sized piece of tenderloin resting on a bed of couscous with a wee bit of chorizo, swimming in butter.

My first divine eating experience there took place but four days after the Vanilla Pod opened. Needless to say, I have returned, again and again. Lunch or dinner, this place delivers a high-quality, mouth-watering culinary experience.

※

And now another treat—more cheese! On Upper Bench Road, a lengthy beige building emerges, smack in the middle of a sizable paved parking lot, complete with a bike rack. But upon closer examination, an intriguing fresco emerges along two walls of the building, the creation of artist Johann Wessels. Fantastic images: cheese and vegetables and dogs and vines, all adding to the ambience of Upper Bench Winery & Creamery.

And the cheese!

Mouthwatering starter at the Vanilla Pod

Although it's not a restaurant, Upper Bench is set up for picnics, and what better choice of food—local cheese. The co-owner and cheese maker, Shana Miller, calls herself the "Big Cheese." Indeed, her repertoire is quite impressive: from a creamy Brie to a tangy washed rind to a sharp, attention-getting blue cheese, the Big Cheese knows what she's doing. Local is as local sources, and these folks get their milk from Sicamous, which is as close as they can manage, considering the volume that they require.

The spacious tasting room offers seven cheeses

and seven wines. They operate on seven acres. Is there some kind of magic going on here? I catch a glimpse of that magic when Shana takes me back into the creamery. Decked out in rubber boots and hairnet, I follow her, careful not to touch anything for fear of contaminating it. Gargantuan barrels for making the cheese, cool rooms for aging and flipping the rounds—sometimes more than once a day—and even cooler rooms for storing all these savoury beauties.

Shana learned her trade at Poplar Grove before launching this dream with her husband, Gavin, who is the winemaker. Shana's cheese and Gavin's wine—a winning combination. The picnic benches out front are a convenient place to unwind with a glass of wine and a cheesy picnic before cycling Upper Bench Road on your way back from the Three Blind Mice or the KVR.

Poplar Grove Cheese
1060 Poplar Grove Road
Penticton, BC

Poplar Grove Winery and Vanilla Pod Restaurant
425 Middle Bench Road North
Penticton, BC

Upper Bench Estate Winery
170 Upper Bench Road South
Penticton, BC

At Poplar Grove Winery (photo courtesy of the McDonald collection)

Upper Bench cheese in the making (photo courtesy of the McDonald collection)

God's Mountain, as seen from across Skaha Lake (photo courtesy of the McDonald collection)

19. Feast of Fields and Joy Road Catering

The name says it all. Feast of Fields is an event that everyone should experience, if only once. At this four-hour wandering harvest festival, with glass and napkin in hand, you can taste the very best from British Columbia's chefs, farmers, fishermen, ranchers, food artisans, vintners, brewers, and distillers. It has been described as a forty-course meal! Feast of Fields events take place throughout the province each year so in order to get in on this, it's best to check their website to find out where the next Okanagan feast will be. Feast of Fields highlights the connections between *local* farmers and chefs, so every feast is different. Their objective is to promote a gastronomic journey toward a sustainable, local food system, something the Slow Food movement has been championing for years.

I've only been to one Feast of Fields, which took place in an apple orchard owned by the Van Westen family on the Naramata Bench. I arrived at the gate, was handed a wineglass and a linen napkin, and was sent off into the orchard to browse. Literally, browse.

Dozens of farmers and chefs and wineries offered delectable bites and sips. The mini-tapas format is ideal because you can sample as much variety as you want, without actually filling up. Delicacies like smoked trout fillets on pumpernickel from Ted's Trout farm, honey-glazed Sterling Springs chicken with a dried apricot and hazelnut crust courtesy of RauDZ Regional Table restaurant in Kelowna, smoked boar hocks with peach salsa or chocolate torte with cherry and plum compote from the Vanilla Pod at Poplar Grove Winery, pulled bison and plum ravioli with peppered saskatoon berry on arugula from the Vintage Room. You get the picture. No toothpick tomatoes here!

After two or three hours, the scene began to resemble a French impressionist painting, with small groups of people sprawled on the grass or perched on bales of hay, talking, nibbling, sipping, sun hats protecting them from the hot Okanagan sun.

Slightly dazed from the food and wine and afternoon heat, the crowds eventually dispersed,

shopping bags filled with tiny samples, recipes, and ideas. Truly a unique and somewhat hedonistic experience.

⟨∿∿⟩

The closest thing to Feast of Fields is something called Joy Road Catering. The owners of Joy Road describe their food as *cuisine du terroir*—food of the earth—which they define as the unique flavour imparted to food or drink by a region's specific climate, soil, weather, and growing conditions—a culinary "sense of place." Joy Road is the brainchild of two young chefs, Cameron Smith and Dana Ewart, whose pedigrees and

training are impeccable. Despite their burnished credentials, their Okanagan careers began at the Penticton Farmers' Market, selling pastries. They believe that using local ingredients makes sense for the simple reason that fresh tastes better. Everyone wins, since their customers enjoy Okanagan products at the height of ripeness and local farmers get to showcase their products.

The young couple's signature gastronomical offering takes place every Sunday evening from May till October each year. It's an intimate (limited to forty people), multi-course vineyard dinner at a dreamy place called God's Mountain Estate, a stunning vineyard positioned on a west-facing bench, high above Skaha Lake. A typical menu might look like this: First course is albacore tartare with lemon aioli, apple and tarragon slaw with grainy Dijon mustard, and purple potato chips. Up next is a bouquet of squash blossoms filled with fresh goat cheese and herbs. Then, scallops and bacon nestled on a bed of creamed corn with marjoram, roasted poblano peppers, and buttermilk onion rings. Still hungry? Hope so, because we're not done yet. Now it's time for house-cured bresaola with shaved pine mushrooms served with wild arugula and a soy and balsamic dressing topped with freshly grated sharp Parmesan. Then comes the heirloom tomato, Italian eggplant, and zucchini ratatouille, or perhaps you'd prefer the braised short rib and seared strip loin with Espelette pepper harissa sauce—or both! All of this, with polenta and rainbow chard.

Dinner is not quite over yet, but we're getting there. The finishing touch is roasted plums with vanilla mascarpone and/or orange blossom olive oil cake and/or golden raspberries and honeycomb. Along with five or six wine pairings, and then a cup of locally roasted coffee or fresh mint tisane, this is the kind of dining experience that, despite the high price, is priceless. The care and attention paid to the food and the wine, the splendid view, the soft caress of the setting sun—it doesn't get any better.

Or maybe it does. On Thursday evenings they present a similar alfresco experience at God's Mountain Estate, but they team up with one of the valley's wineries. This is a chance to actually meet the featured winemaker and learn about the wines, all the while enjoying the delicious food and the ambience of the spectacular location. In both cases, their website is the place to go to learn about their next dinner.

FarmFolk CityFolk Feast of Fields
www.feastoffields.com

Joy Road Catering
www.joyroadcatering.com

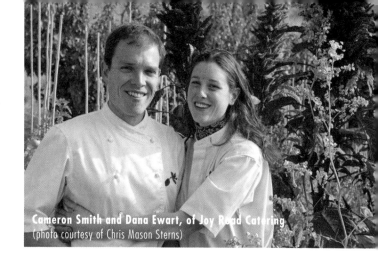

Cameron Smith and Dana Ewart, of Joy Road Catering
(photo courtesy of Chris Mason Sterns)

Karolina Born-Tschümperlin selling her Forest Green Man Lavender products at Feast of Fields in Winfield in 2013
(photo courtesy of Doug Mathias)

Entrance to Ruby Blues Winery

20. Naramata Bench Wine

Gnarled orchards, orderly vineyards dotted with wineries, and a dead-end road. With its gently sloping, west-facing fields that dip and bend to the shores of Okanagan Lake, the Naramata Bench has a certain bucolic beauty. There are dozens of things to do and see up on "the Bench," as it's known, but it is most famous for its wineries: twenty-four at last count. Here are a few standouts that merit a visit.

As you head north on Naramata Road, take care not to miss La Frenz Winery. A little tricky to find, it requires a hard right turn off Naramata Road onto modest Randolph Road, and then a left into the winery parking lot. For wine enthusiasts, this is the place to come for consistent quality and sheer drinkability. I don't know of another winery in the South Okanagan, or perhaps the entire Okanagan, that has garnered as many well-deserved awards as La Frenz. Basically, my motto is that if it's from La Frenz, just drink it!

I always chuckle when I arrive at La Frenz. There is no showroom. The wines are tucked behind the counter so you can't fondle them. There is no gift shop. There are no books, placemats, crackers, calendars, corkscrews, or tea towels. The tasting counter is quite small. And the lineup is always long. La Frenz is all about wine. That's it.

Niva and Jeff Martin are the owners, the growers, the winemakers, the marketers, and the sellers. Hailing from the Riverina area of Australia, they have been involved with grape-growing and winemaking since early childhood. It shows. From Australia they moved to the Napa Valley, then to Quails' Gate Winery near Kelowna, and finally to the Naramata Bench.

La Frenz might be the most difficult place in the entire valley from which to choose favourites, but if I had to, I would probably pick their Viognier and Shiraz. Or maybe the Sauvignon Blanc. If you can get your hands on a bottle—or a case—of any of their wines, I would suggest doing so. You can drink the first bottle, with whatever delectable nibbly you've brought from town, out on their picnic patio overlooking one of their vineyards, and pack the other eleven in the car.

La Frenz Winery

The next featured winery along this journey is Red Rooster. One of the most impressive winery buildings in the entire Okanagan, it has wood salvaged from the original Naramata train dock incorporated into the soaring arched doorways of the tasting room. Red Rooster is passionate about art. It's everywhere: from the sculpture garden surrounding the building (which includes *"Frank" the Baggage Handler*) to the art on the walls throughout the tasting room to an entire second-floor gallery.

Across the street is Ruby Blues, perhaps the winery with the cheekiest attitude. You pull into the parking lot and unfold yourself from your car to have the unmistakable sounds of the Rolling Stones greet you. No, you haven't had too much wine. There are speakers, camouflaged in the vineyard, blasting out Mick at his best. Then there is the psychedelic Volkswagen van at the entrance, along with the wild and colourful frescos on the winery's external walls and more rich and decadent colours in the interior. Their tasting fee is—wait for it—a smile! Yes, this winery definitely has a sense of humour. Except when it comes to their wines. On that point they're very serious.

A short distance up the road is Hillside Winery. It began as an apricot orchard in the early 1900s, but in 1979, Bohumir and Vera Klokocka, recent immigrants from Czechoslovakia, purchased the property with a dream—orderly rows of grapes that would become outstanding wine. They planted their first grapes in 1984 and released their first vintage—a mere twenty-five cases—in 1989, making Hillside one of the first farm-gate wineries in British Columbia.

The current building was the first winery designed by renowned architect Robert Mackenzie, in 1997. The timber-frame building is inspired by a gristmill design, with a twenty-two-metre tower that is as functional as it is impressive, since it serves as a ventilation shaft to cool the winery cellar in the hot summer months. The original farmhouse is now the tasting room. Surrounding the winery are colourful gardens with more than a hundred plant species, cascading down a slope.

Red Rooster Winery

Apart from the wines, now upwards of ten thousand cases a year, another great reason to stop at Hillside, either by car from Naramata Road or—even better—by bike from the Kettle Valley Railway, which skims the upper edge of the winery, is the restaurant. Lunch and dinner are both available, and although the menu isn't extensive, it's selective and good. The braised Fraser Valley pork cheeks, served with maple butter–roasted pears, Belgian endive, blue cheese, potato, and pecans, are perfectly paired with Hillside's Old Vines Gamay Noir. This is a medium-bodied, fruit-forward wine with a fine silky texture, the product of the knobby and twisted, over-thirty-year-old Gamay vines that are visible as you enter the restaurant. Gamay Noir is not commonly found in the South Okanagan, and Hillside does it very well.

Continuing up the road, you soon come to Laughing Stock Vineyards. These guys have a great tongue-in-cheek attitude about life, wine, and business. Maybe that's because of their previous careers in the financial industry. They've brought some of that culture with them, with taglines like "assets," "portfolios," and "blind trusts." It may sound slightly corny, but when it comes to making wine, David and Cynthia Enns are serious.

Hillside Winery

In 2003, they left a life that was comfortable and familiar, and invested bullishly in the wine industry. It was an emotional decision that has turned out extremely well for them—and for anyone who can get their hands on their wine. It's hard to choose a favourite from this pair of pros,

but their flagship wine, the Portfolio, stands out. This Bordeaux blend has developed into a world-class wine that garners awards and recognition wherever it is consumed.

Not content to simply grow grapes, make wine, and sell it, this couple has embraced the valley in all its forms and taken up skiing, snowboarding, biking, and stand-up paddle boarding. It's not unusual on a warm summer morning to catch a glimpse of two Adonis-like figures gliding silently and smoothly across the bay. None other than David and Cynthia Enns on their paddle boards.

Black Widow Winery may not have the friendliest name, but the owners defend their label convincingly, pointing out that the desert climate in which they grow grapes is also home to the furry black creature with the red bum. Black Widow wines are vineyard-exclusive, which means every single grape used to make them is grown on the Naramata Bench. Their Pinot Gris, Syrah, and Rosé are well worth the trip, and the black widow–inspired bike rack out front gives a friendly nod to the increasing number of customers who are self-propelled.

One of the more recent wineries to appear on the Bench is Terravista Vineyards, up on Sutherland Road. But don't be fooled by the newness of the winery. The co-owner and winemaker is none other than Senka Tennant, of Nota Bene fame. Originally from Croatia, Senka moved to Canada with her family at the age of fourteen. She was a teacher before she and her husband joined forces with another couple in 1995 to purchase the land where Black Hills Estate Winery now stands. It was merely desert then, but the four planted more than twenty-six acres of vines. For their first vintage, in 1999, they hired a winemaker from Washington State, but after that Senka took over. She mastered the nuances quickly and soon began producing stupendous wine. When the famously fussy wine critic Anthony Gismondi awarded her a ninety-three for one of her vintages, she laughed it off. "I think he must have been high on Chablis or something when he gave me that rating."

After the sale of Black Hills, Senka and her husband, Bob, realized they weren't quite finished with making wine. Calling herself a "cellar rat," she began searching with Bob for a piece of land on which they could grow grapes and make wine. They found four acres of it on Sutherland Road. They weren't interested in replicating what they had done down south, so they planted two varietals that originate in the Galicia region of Spain: Albariño and Verdejo. Concentrating now on only two wines, Figaro and Fandango, Senka is passionate about the quality of the fruit. "My job is to express the growing season," she says. "I don't want to muck with it too much, but I do want to make delicious wine." And she does. A short bike ride up Sutherland Road from where the KVR crosses it, Terravista has a low-key style that is refreshing.

Lake Breeze is probably the most beautifully situated winery on the entire Naramata Bench. After you drop down from Naramata Road, the

Terravista Vineyards

Breeze, the Terravista dog

winery emerges, disarmingly similar to those in South Africa—all cottagey and whitewashed. There is a logical explanation. In 1995, Paul and Vereena Moser, a Swiss couple who had lived in South Africa for twenty-five years, bought a twelve-acre parcel of land on the Naramata Bench called Rock Oven Vineyards. The winery was built in the Cape Dutch style in 1996 and christened Lake Breeze for obvious reasons. They were the first to plant Pinotage, a native South African varietal created from crossing Pinot Noir and Cinsaut.

The second South African connection is Garron Elmes, the winemaker who has been with the winery since its inception. Garron was born in Capetown, South Africa, and earned his winemaking stripes in the famed Stellenbosch region. This is another winery that offers a plethora of fine wines, their refreshing Pinot Blanc and truly luscious Seven Poplars Pinot Noir being favourites. Or, wait—how about the Pinotage? It's one of their signature wines. And the Sauvignon Blanc. Once again, it's too difficult to choose.

This winery is worth a visit—for the wine to

be sure, but also for lunch! Outdoor seating only. Local ingredients only. Lake Breeze wine pairings only. First come, first served only. Come early and stay late. Chef Mark Ashton was trained in France, offers a Mediterranean style of cooking, and is committed to the local ingredients of the Okanagan Valley.

JoieFarm Winery, near the village of Naramata, is owned and operated by Heidi Noble and Michael Dinn. *Joie* is the French word for joy, which is what this enterprise has brought to the lives of the owners, and to anyone who has tasted their wines. Their business model is unusual, for they don't actually have a tasting room! And yet their wines are famous. How does that happen, and how do you get your hands on one of their wines? It's simple, as it turns out. Head down to the Naramata General Store, and voila! There they are. Check the wine list at any restaurant featuring Western Canadian fine wines, and there they are again. JoieFarm specializes in the grape varieties of Alsace and Burgundy, which seem to excel in the cool-climate desert landscape of the Okanagan Valley. The Noble Blend is the most famous: 43 percent Gewürztraminer, 38 percent Riesling, 14 percent Pinot Auxerrois, and 5 percent Pinot Gris. Winemaker, chef, sommelier, and author Heidi Noble combines these grapes to create a beautifully balanced and complex white wine.

Gate at the entrance to Lake Breeze Vineyards

La Frenz Winery
1525 Randolph Road
Penticton, BC

Red Rooster Winery
891 Naramata Road
Penticton, BC

Ruby Blues Winery
917 Naramata Road
Penticton, BC

Hillside Winery
1350 Naramata Road
Penticton, BC

Laughing Stock Vineyards
1548 Naramata Road
Penticton, BC

Black Widow Winery
1630 Naramata Road
Penticton, BC

Terravista Vineyards
1853 Sutherland Road
Penticton, BC

Lake Breeze Vineyards
930 Sammet Road
Naramata, BC

JoieFarm Winery
www.joiefarm.com

Entrance to Elephant Island Orchard Wines

21. Aikins Loop

While relaxing in the cool, shaded courtyard at Elephant Island Orchard Wines, I asked owner Miranda Halladay how she came to this marvellous place.

"See these trees?" she replied. I glanced up at the massive oaks and maples providing us with ample shade. "They were just twigs in the ground when I first arrived."

"Impossible," I exclaimed. "They must be sixty years old—or older."

Miranda explained that they were actually nearer to forty, planted when she first came here to play in her grandparents' orchard.

This fruit winery began its life as a family orchard. Miranda's grandparents came from Chojnów in southern Poland. They escaped from the work camps in Spain where they had been sent, immigrated to North America, and kept going west until there was nowhere left to go. British Columbia welcomed them and they responded by working hard. While Miranda's architect grandmother designed and built a futuristic home on the property, complete with outdoor kitchen and solar power, Granddad planted a cherry orchard. Although he planted it primarily for fruit production, he never forgot his Polish roots and was soon making wine out of those very same fruits.

At about the time the orchard became too much work for her aging grandparents, Miranda and her husband, Mel, came along with the idea of turning the orchard into a fruit winery. Granddad had left detailed notes about the process, so they simply needed to acquire the proper equipment for commercial production. Everything seemed to be falling into place.

Then tragedy struck. Their baby son, Rex, died suddenly and unexpectedly. To honour his memory they created Little King—a champagne-style wine with a hint of strawberry. That and a pink champagne they call Pink Elephant remain their most popular wines.

The winery is on the Aikins Loop road, another biking mecca. As you wheel into the tasting room area, the atmosphere is welcoming, casual, and

Elephant Island Orchard Wines
2730 Aikins Loop
Naramata, BC

Van Westen Vineyards
2800A Aikins Loop
Naramata, BC

friendly. Immediately beyond the tasting room is that shady courtyard, with a small fountain burbling away, round tables and chairs providing the perfect setting for a picnic lunch and another glass of bubbly. A kids' area welcomes the younger set, and Grandma's house is still there, at the edge of the courtyard.

Three generations.

Around the corner on the Aikins Loop road is another family establishment that dabbles in both fruit and wine. More than dabbles. The Van Westen family has been farming here for more than fifty years. With extensive apple and cherry orchards, plus vineyards to supply their family estate winery, the Van Westens are one busy family. Winemaker Robert Van Westen clearly knows his business because his wines are winning prestigious prizes. In particular, the Merlot / Cabernet Franc blend, aptly called Voluptuous, has won many awards. This is a big, velvety, almost smoky red wine. Another winner is their Vino Grigio, a surprisingly complex wine that starts softly and ends with a nice citrus kick. The concrete bunker appearance of the Van Westen winery probably won't inspire huge accolades, but the wines more than make up for it.

Pedalling around this quaint agricultural area among these unique winemaking establishments makes the experience even better.

A veritable feast!

Forest Green Man Lavender Farm

22. Forest Green Man Lavender Farm

The first time I visited the lavender farm I knew two things about lavender: it was purple, and it smelled great. I'm still no expert, but after a few years of visiting the farm and helping out with various stages of production, I realize there's a lot more to lavender than simply stuffing your nose into it. You can bathe in it, rub your headachy temples with it, decorate your house with it, or place a few drops of the oil on your pillow to sleep with it. You can even eat it!

Still, the overwhelming impression upon entering the lavender farm is that it is unbelievably purple and even more aromatic. The undulating slopes, with their rows of flawlessly sculpted mounds, are a sight to behold. Upon closer inspection of those slender silvery leaves and millions of purple blossoms, you realize that not all the rows are alike. Now the lavender education begins.

But first, a word about the name of this place. Forest Green Man is a stylized face of leaves and branches—an ancient Celtic spirit of nature that symbolizes growth, fertility, and renewal. Here at the farm, it represents not only lavender, but also sour cherries and Ambrosia apples, Italian prune plums and Russian red garlic, all of which are grown in different nooks and crannies of the farm. In the garden next to the bright orange guest cottage, you can find rows of heirloom tomatoes and luscious raspberries. Gigantic blackberries drape over their supporting trellises nearby.

A feeling of permanence emanates from Forest Green Man, a reflection of its hundred-year history as a producing farm. The soil is rich and fertile. The funky, brightly coloured buildings complement the landscape. Co-owner Doug Mathias's family has farmed this land for fifty years, first as an orchard. Now, he and his Swiss-born wife, Karolina Born-Tschümperlin, are concentrating increasingly on lavender.

Back to the lavender. Karolina explains that although all lavender varieties are edible, some taste a little soapy so they are not used for cooking. Two tasty varieties of culinary lavender are Munstead and the pink-hued Mellisa. With a mere hint of

Lavender field in Provence in all its summer splendor

The most common lavender varieties used for non-culinary products are Grosso and Provence, both of which have a soapy, clean, slightly medicinal scent. This is the lavender that forms those armloads of fresh-cut bouquets that you see at farmers' markets each week or here at the lavender store. It can also be dried and removed from the stems to make tiny aromatic sachets and eye pillows.

But there is one product that tops them all—lavender essential oil. To create the oil a completely different process is used, one with which I became intimately familiar by helping out at the farm. I often wondered why lavender oil was so expensive. Now I know.

First, the lavender must be harvested by hand. Next, it is carted in wheelbarrows from the field up to a copper still. Armloads of lavender are stuffed into the top container of the still, then the lid is pushed down and sealed with a rye-flour paste in order to trap the steam. The bottom of the still holds boiling water, which produces the steam that rises through a copper column. The steam breaks down the cells in the lavender stalks and flowers, releasing the essential oil, which is then carried by the steam into a copper coil. There, the steam condenses and carries the hydrosol containing the essential oil into the *essencier*. The essencier is a separator that allows the essential oil to float on top of the distilled

sweetness, they add a dreamy flavour to crème brûlée or lavender shortbread. Culinary lavender is also pesticide-free, harvested by hand, and sold in food-safe containers. The harvesting process is a buzzing affair for hundreds, if not thousands, of honeybees hover about as you snip away at the flowers. The trick is to stay calm and watch where you put your hands! After it's harvested and tied in bunches, it is hung to dry for approximately fifteen days. The lavender buds are then hand removed from the stems and eventually sifted in order to remove all the little bits of leaf and stem that might remain. Now the lavender is ready to be combined with other culinary items such as salt, pepper, herbs grown on the farm, vinegar, jelly, or honey.

water and be collected. This—finally—is lavender oil. Thick, aromatic, and distilled right here on the farm. The ratio of water to oil is 100:1! The remaining hydrosol in the essencier is the source of lavender water; those precious drops of oil are also used to scent bath salts and soap.

The entire distilling process takes place outside the little yellow barn that serves as a shop, among other things. Eclectic and slightly chaotic, the shop is filled with delightful temptations: lavender products that are made on the farm, plus gorgeous tablecloths from the south of France, dried cherries and apricots, pashmina shawls from Kashmir, paintings, and cookbooks. And on a hot sunny day, you can enjoy a glass of lavender lemonade outside under a brightly painted umbrella, surrounded by flowers, next to a gushing fountain.

If it's too difficult to leave this idyllic little place, it's also possible to spend the night. That orange-and-blue cottage perched at the top of the lavender field is for rent. With a fully equipped kitchen and a deck overlooking the fields of bloom and the lake in the distance, vegetables a few steps away and wineries up the road, it seems like a logical place to stay awhile.

Forest Green Man Lavender Farm
620 Boothe Road
Naramata, BC

Lavender essential oil in the making

Otis, "farm dog extraordinaire"

One of Naramata's own peacocks

23. Naramata Village

The village of Naramata is a curious little place. Maybe it's due to the origin of its name, which was allegedly the result of a spiritualist seance. Founded in 1907, Naramata began as an agricultural community but, unusual for that time, was also known in its early years as a cultural centre. People from up and down the Okanagan Valley would arrive by paddlewheeler at the Naramata wharf and flock to the village for concerts and plays—even operas. The isolated nature of the village changed in 1914 when the Kettle Valley Railway was finally completed on the steep, rocky hillside high above the town. A road eventually followed and more people discovered this quaint end-of-the-line village.

Okanagan Lake dominates the scene, but on the back streets tiny cottages are tucked away, almost hidden among the verdant foliage. Mature trees flourish and the gardens are lush and productive. Peacocks wander by. Vineyards dot the rolling landscape, as do a few remnant orchards. An occasional mansion peers out from the landscaping, usually presiding over a grand lake view.

The village of Naramata is part of a movement that is the essence of slow. *Cittaslow*, the Italian phrase for a slow city or town, is an international network. In order to qualify as a cittaslow, a community must commit itself to improving the quality of life for its citizens, protecting the environment, promoting local goods and products, and avoiding the sameness that is a scourge the world over. The movement has strong links to Slow Food and includes towns in England, Norway, Poland, and Portugal. The good people of Naramata have been one of these cittaslows since 2010. Wonderful initiative!

Naramata's Robinson Avenue is possibly the quietest main street in the entire Okanagan Valley. Quiet and slow. A village highlight is the Centre at Naramata, a conference-and-retreat facility operated by the United Church of Canada. Their mandate is simple: inspire people to make a difference in the world. The grounds of the centre feature

Naramata Heritage Inn & Spa

a natural grass-and-stone labyrinth. There is no "right" way to walk the labyrinth, but walking it is a meditative experience. Also gracing the property is the elegant post-and-beam Chalmers Chapel, designed for worship, meditation, or performance. I once sat, mesmerized, through a four-hour sitar concert in the Chalmers Chapel.

For a less structured experience you can swim, paddle board or kayak on the lake, cycle along the KVR above town, shop at the farmers' market each Wednesday afternoon, or eat. Yes, eat. There are several options in town, including the funky little Café Nevermatters smack in the "busiest" part of downtown. With a spacious outdoor area and cozy interior, this little establishment is usually packed.

One of the leaders in the local slow movement is the Naramata Heritage Inn & Spa. Committed to the Italian expression *festina lente*, which means hasten slowly, the inn promotes life on a human scale while simultaneously harnessing the best aspects of technology. A tricky balancing act.

The slower pace is immediately apparent as you pull into the driveway of the Naramata Heritage Inn. Enormous shade trees dwarf the tiny parking lot. This gracious California-inspired hotel has been around since 1908, built by the village founder, John Moore Robinson. It was his private residence, then a girls' school, and finally a hotel, which has been lovingly restored to provide a unique combination of Old World elegance and modern comfort. The inn oozes charm: glistening hardwood floors, solid beams overhead, double-hung windows, cozy brick-lined fireplaces, and comfy antiques in every corner. The dining experience here is superb, with the freshest of vegetables, many from their own garden, local wines, and a very fine chef, Alexander K. Campbell. This is a quiet get-away kind of place that soothes, pampers, and delights in equal measures.

The Centre at Naramata
3375 3rd Street
Naramata, BC

Café Nevermatters
340 Robinson Avenue
Naramata, BC

Naramata Heritage Inn & Spa
3625 1st Street
Naramata, BC

At Mill Bay

"Downtown" Naramata welcomes you!

Welcome to...
"Naramata Village"

↑ NARAMATA STORE
↑ SUN N' SUP STAND UP PADDLE BOARDING
↑ SHADES OF LINEN CLOTHING
CARLARRY GLASS ART
3545 - 3RD St.
← LONE JONES PHOTOGRAPHY
⚓ ROYAL ANCHOR RESORT →
LAVENDER FARM
Turn Right at Anna Ave. →
SANDY BEACH LODGE & RESORT
Turn Right at Anna Ave. Follow onto Mill Rd. →
HAIR STUDIO
Kathy 496-4247 →

Canoeing on Okanagan Lake

24. Paddling in Okanagan Lake Provincial Park

A canoe is a beautiful piece of equipment—sleek, smooth, and practical, with no moving parts. It comes alive in the water, responding instantly to whatever a stream or lake offers up. It cuts through gentle ripples of water with little effort, then twitches and shudders in the nervous chop caused by a freshening wind and differing depths of water. As the waves increase in size, it pitches and rolls before carving a path through the near-vertical walls of water. At least that's the idea.

Okanagan Lake is a very large lake, and from time to time, it can be affected by extremely strong winds. As a result, the waves can be large, rolling, and topped with a foam of white. So it's important to be vigilant in monitoring the weather on this lake. But it's worth it, because paddling a canoe on a still morning, slicing through the glassy waters in complete solitude, is a magnificent way to start the day.

There is a poetry of motion when, paddling with your entire body, you move through the water in unison with your partner. The shoreline slips by, one kilometre at a time. Steep clay cliffs riddled with bank swallow nests give way to grasslands studded with the occasional ponderosa pine. A bald eagle perches on the highest point, craning its neck first left, then right, searching for fish far below. Families of ducks scoot by, their tiny legs paddling as fast as they can, trying to get out of the way. Overhanging walls of ancient gneiss abut the translucent water, providing shaded enclaves of coolness.

Stroke after stroke, our paddles cut the water and the canoe glides forward. The unrelenting Okanagan sun beats down, reflected by this immense body of water. Then, just beyond a cliff is a tiny perfect beach, private and pristine. Overheated from paddling, we drift in, step out of the canoe into the warm shallows, and pull the boat up onto shore. A minute later we're back in the water, swimming out into the ridiculously clear, impossibly blue lake, cool and refreshed.

There are dozens of such beaches, countless clay cliffs, eagles, and ducks along the eastern

Hidden rock caves on Okanagan Lake, accessible by canoe (photo courtesy of the McDonald collection)

Stand-up paddle boarding (photo courtesy of Cornelia Vock)

shore of the lake in Okanagan Lake Provincial Park. You can paddle for a morning—or for a week. Campsites along the way have everything you could need: a flat place to set up a tent, firepits for cooking or for a cheery evening fire, toilets, and always, pristine, untouched beaches.

This is a part of the Okanagan Valley that few people see, and it's a shame because the lake is not solely for the enjoyment of the motorboat crowd. Particularly out toward the centre of the lake the wind can be squirrelly, and it picks up very quickly. But there's always a cove or bay into which you can dart, to take cover for a few minutes or an hour while a squall passes through.

We are more accustomed to looking down at this lake, admiring its colour and size and the fact that it dominates and defines the valley. We might visit a city beach or bike along a trail, but to actually be *in* this huge body of water, away from the crowds and exploring its untouched shores under our own power, is to see it from a completely different angle. Gazing across at towns and roads and vineyards and orchards, but from the peace and quiet of an undeveloped shoreline: this is wilderness in the heart of the valley.

A writer in her element!
(photo courtesy of the
McDonald collection)

Meadowlarks and
sunflowers

25. Summerland Ornamental Gardens

A somewhat imposing structure presides over the bench above Okanagan Lake, immediately south of Summerland. The Summerland Agricultural Research Centre is a vitally important organization that has helped shape the direction of agriculture in this valley. Adjacent to the research centre, and a short distance up the hill, are the Summerland Ornamental Gardens—fifteen acres of heaven.

A peaceful, restful green enclave, the gardens are studded with lofty, stately ponderosa pines. Rolling lawns rimmed with formal flower beds conjure up a different era and a more relaxed schedule, when there was time to think, have a picnic, visit with family and friends.

Trails lead along the top of a canyon, to the rose garden, and across expansive lawns. There are all kinds of events and activities to participate in, from painting classes to formal teas, but the best way to experience the gardens, in my opinion, is simply to go there with some time. Walk. Sit. Look. Smell.

But wait. This place is not all about flowers and grass. Something else is percolating at the Summerland gardens. The xeriscape garden, a relatively new addition, is a labour of love for Eva Antonijevic. Eva, the community program director for the Friends of Summerland Ornamental Gardens, is utterly suited for this mammoth task. She is experienced in urban natural habitat restoration and natural garden ecosystems, as well as environmental stewardship. There is nothing she loves more than introducing native plants to a garden. They help to create ecological micro-habitats that support local insects, butterflies, and birds.

When Eva began working at the Summerland Ornamental Gardens there were very few native plants in the xeriscape garden, which occupies two and a half acres of the total site. With new water conservation efforts now in place, she and the other Friends have committed to increasing the number of native plants, as this is one of the best ways to reduce water needs. They recently planted more than thirty-five hundred native plants with the help of a hundred and twenty students from

Superintendent's House at Summerland Ornamental Gardens

five local schools. Students from the Penticton Indian Band's alternative school created a list of Nsyilxcen (the local First Nation language) names for all the species of native plants that they planted, which will be labelled side by side with the common and botanical names.

And although this is now the largest xeriscape garden of its kind in Canada, the work is

Xeriscape garden project

far from over. They continue to introduce more native plants, as well as more drought-tolerant non-native plants, into the overall gardens, which cover a huge area. Eventually the lawn areas will be replaced with eco-lawns, which require less water and maintenance. It's clear to the custodians that the current plantings are not sustainable, so the strategy is to rethink, replant, and redesign the garden. Each of these incremental changes is combined with solid horticultural education that makes sense today. The Summerland Ornamental Gardens are a fascinating place to see and experience a nineteenth-century garden evolving into one of the twenty-first century.

Summerland Ornamental Gardens
4200 Highway 97
Summerland, BC

A glass full of bubbles from 8th Generation Vineyard . . . yes, please!

26. 8th Generation and a Glass Full of Bubbles

Prosecco surely must be one of the essential food groups. Its bubbly tartness is the ideal way to introduce a meal, welcome guests, or enhance a conversation. We can be thankful that 8th Generation Vineyard in Summerland understands this basic fact.

Bernd and Stefanie Schales, owners of 8th Generation, come from a long winemaking lineage: Bernd is an eighth-generation winemaker, and Stefanie's family has been growing grapes for ten generations. Winemaking has been a continuous tradition in their families for over two hundred and twenty-five years, so when they moved from Germany to the Okanagan they brought their Old World methods to the New World.

Architecturally trained Stefanie might have chosen something different for the actual winery building, which is not the most attractive. But it's what's inside that counts: everything from an antique wine press that belonged to Bernd's grandfather to the most sophisticated computer-controlled fillers. And the wine.

Their portfolio is huge and somewhat overwhelming in scope. One of the best Rieslings in the valley, their Riesling Classic comes from twenty-five-year-old vines and has a tantalizing taste combo of lemon and apple. Vancouver wine critic Anthony Gismondi calls it a "Riesling for grownups."[1]

But my hands-down favourite is their Integrity Prosecco. Made of 65 percent Chardonnay and 35 percent Pinot Gris, this wine is always in my fridge. (Not the same bottle, needless to say.) With tiny, gentle explosions, the bubbles burst by the thousands. This is a young wine with powerful hints of pear and apple and pineapple. When they first moved here from Germany, Stefanie was puzzled to find that nobody in the Okanagan was making Prosecco. It was obviously popular, since the liquor stores sold numerous European brands, so why nothing local? As she logically pointed out, "It is so popular—you have it at least once a week."

Indeed! The numbers prove her point. Sales of Prosecco in Canada skyrocketed 266 percent in the four-year period ending September 2010, with annual sales reaching 111,238 nine-litre cases. Even during the recession, volume sold over the past two years soared 49 percent.

And it's not just Canada that loves Prosecco. It is so popular in some places in Italy that it's served like beer, on tap: *Prosecco alla spina.*

In case drinking straight Prosecco once a week is too much, here is Stefanie's recipe for her Hugo cocktail:

1 to 2 tablespoons elderflower syrup
3 mint leaves, rubbed to release the oils
8th Generation Integrity Prosecco, to top

Pour the syrup into a wineglass. Drop in the mint leaves, and top with Integrity Prosecco.

The Schales family is not content to let things rest with this generation. They are nurturing their children, teaching them the craft of winemaking and how to care for the land, in the hopes that the 9th Generation Vineyard will be even better than the 8th.

8th Generation Vineyard
6807 Highway 97
Summerland, BC

Wine selection at 8th Generation

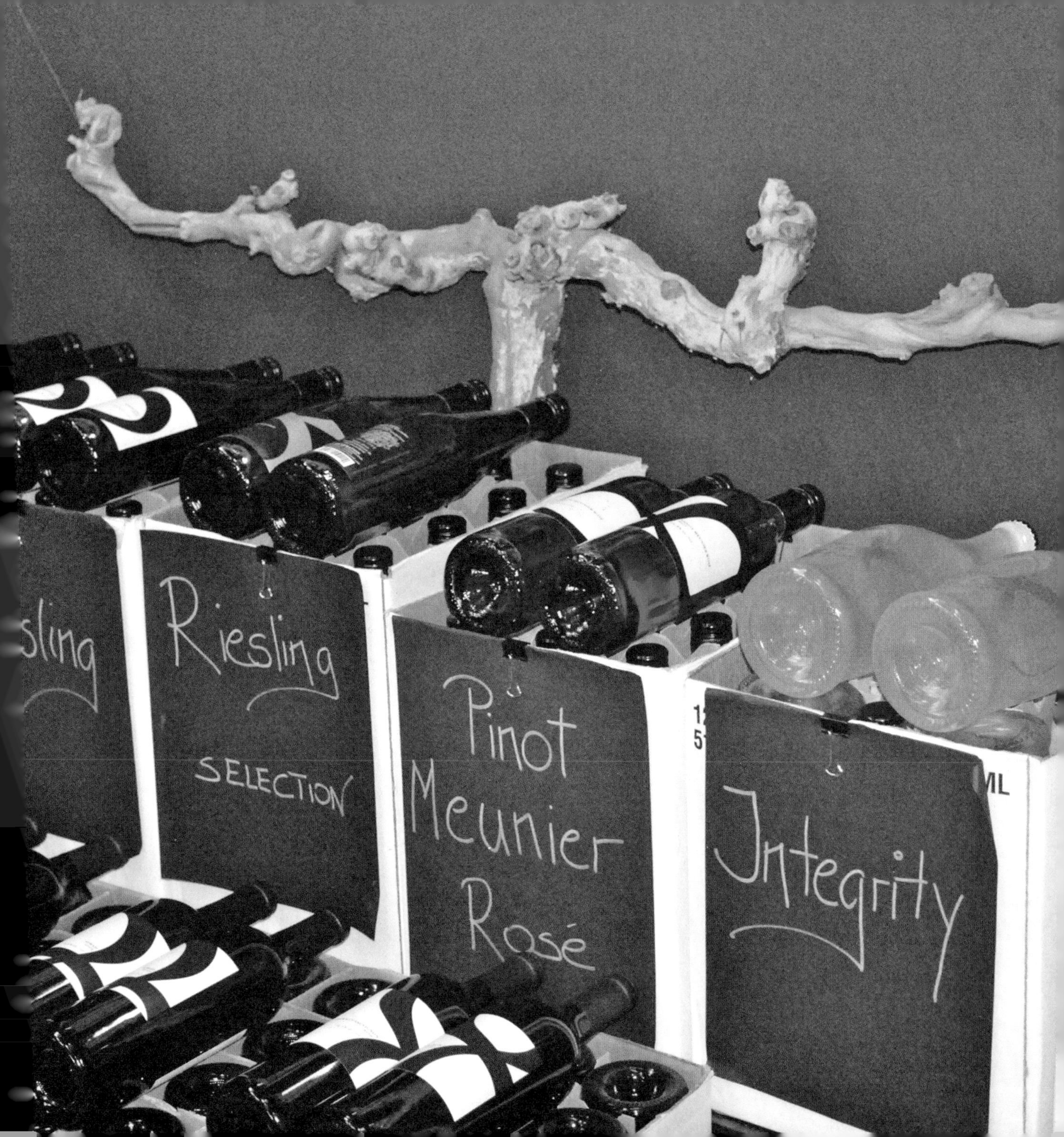
sling
Riesling
SELECTION
Pinot
Meunier
Rosé
Integrity
ML

Kettle Valley Railway locomotive

27. Summerland Hills

The town of Summerland lies in a caldera, a basin-like depression that resulted when an ancient volcano exploded. Summerland's major landmark is Giant's Head Mountain, a volcanic plug right in the middle of town. Every possible piece of land that surrounds the town is farmed—there are orchards, market gardens, and vineyards. Fir- and pine-covered slopes cascade down to these agricultural areas, while precipitous clay cliffs and narrow gulches plunge to the lake below. In Summerland, if it's not vertical, it's probably a farm: this community is seriously committed to agriculture.

At first glance it appears a sleepy little town, a great place to sample some superb organic bread or enjoy an alfresco gourmet lunch. But there's more here than meets the eye. There are some fantastic opportunities to stretch the legs and lungs. For starters, there is the obvious choice—Giant's Head Mountain. To make the ascent by car, you have to take a narrow, twisting road that crawls up the southern slope of the mountain. It's possible to drive maddeningly close to the top,

which is somewhat unfortunate since it would be much nicer if there wasn't a road at all. But it's not absolutely mandatory that you drive that road. A number of trails start at the bottom of the mountain and it's much more rewarding to hike up the hill than to drive. Or you could pedal your bike up those switchbacks to earn the view at the top.

The summit, with its wind-sculpted ponderosa pines and Douglas firs, is usually buffeted by a fresh breeze. Strange little directional metal tubes help focus the eyes on nearby mountains, down to the southern shores of Okanagan Lake, and up into the Prairie Valley in the west. You can observe tiny sailboats battling gusty winds or gaze across the east side of the lake to the agricultural patchwork quilt of the Naramata Bench. It's all so far down because the summit is so far up! It feels even higher when you stare down the cliffs on the north side. Yes. A real mountain! Now, if you've opted for a bike for the ascent, it's a breathless scream as you race down the road, banking steeply around each tight curve.

Around the back of Giant's Head Mountain,

View from the Test of Humanity trail above Summerland
(photo courtesy of the McDonald collection)

you can follow the signs to the Trans Canada Trail. The Fenwick Road trailhead is a good place to begin this enticing trail, which is best enjoyed on a mountain bike. Although loosely associated with the historic Kettle Valley Railway, this trail is a little different. For one thing, it is hilly. And to start things off, there are a couple of steep turns to climb, to get above the private properties and onto the trail proper. Up and down, around and over, the double-wide trail is a pleasure to ride, with rewarding views of the pastoral prettiness of the Prairie Valley, filled with orchards, horse farms, and hay ranches. Below the trail is the actual KVR,

along which the steam-powered Kettle Valley train still chugs. A conveniently placed trailside viewpoint, complete with a little gazebo, offers an eagle's-eye view down onto the train as it puffs past, whistle blowing. Riding through this open ponderosa pine grassland is great fun, culminating at the Prairie Valley station, where, if you're lucky, the train is in, all black and gleaming and sleek.

If this ride is too easy, and for many it probably is, there is an alternative with an intriguing name: Test of Humanity. Local rock climbers and cyclists Nic and Sheri Seaton—the brains behind this challenging bike route—had an unusual vision.

In addition to piecing together a collection of old, unconnected trails, they have created a race, also called the Test of Humanity, that is a fundraiser for Canadian humanitarian work in Ethiopia. Their objective is to raise enough money to break the cycle of poverty and illiteracy for orphaned children there. Information about the race is on their website but there's no need to race to enjoy the route they have created.

This roller-coaster bike route is 9.75 kilometres in length, with approximately 85 percent of the course being single track. There are nine hills and 280 metres of climbing throughout the course, which means that moderate-to-expert skills are required, along with a good set of lungs. With a mix of pine forest and open grassland, this exciting trail features banked downhill corners and endless switchbacks. Evocative locator names like Lactic Acid Test, Boulder Garden, Compression Col, and Hike a Bike give an idea of the terrain. In some spots, alternate routes are available (Cardiac Bypass vs. Cardiac Arrest). But the best of all the names has to be Bust a Gut.

It's unusual to have a bike route of this quality available in the middle of a town, and when you combine it with the Trans Canada Trail and Giant's Head Mountain, there is no excuse to be slothful in Summerland!

Cycling the Test of Humanity
(photo courtesy of the McDonald collection)

The Giant's Head Mountain trailhead is 100 m up Milne Road at Giant's Head Road in Summerland, BC.

The Test of Humanity trailhead is on Prairie Valley Road in Summerland, BC.

Both of these trails are less than half-day outings. Great to combine with some of the other treats that Summerland has on offer.

True Grain Bread (photo courtesy of the McDonald collection)

28. Culinary Summerland

Word began circulating that there was a new "it" bakery in Summerland. Artisan. Out-of-this-world bread. Rumour had it that they were even grinding their own flour. Better check it out.

There, on Main Street, in a storefront where bakeries have been operating since the 1940s, was a place called True Grain Bread. I peered through the window and came face to face with attractive displays of golden brown loaves, whole grain loaves, round loaves, oblong loaves, seed-studded loaves, long crusty loaves, flat olive-stuffed ciabattas. I opened the door and was assaulted by the most alluring aroma.

My timing was flawless. At around 10:00 in the morning the shelves were bursting with beauty and I felt as though I had arrived in heaven. Well, except for that irritatingly long lineup of customers buying bags full of bread and cinnamon rolls, and ruining the display. But as luck would have it, enormous trays laden with warm, fresh, and equally beautiful loaves were marched out of the kitchen as quickly as the shelves emptied. What a scene—a caravan of bread!

What was the story here? I asked the young lady behind the display. She directed me to the owner, Todd Laidlaw, who was busy in the kitchen. Out he bounded, young and energetic and friendly, keen to tell the story of his bakery, which is actually a partnership with another bakery in Cowichan Bay on Vancouver Island. Todd explained that he isn't the baker—that honour rests with their *Bäckermeister*, a master baker from Germany. Why Germany? I asked. Because that's the style of baking that True Grain Bread prefers—hearty, whole-grained European breads.

So what was Todd's role, other than owning the place? He smiled and took me over to a giant window opening onto a small room in which stood an unusual-looking machine. Stunning piece of technology. All bleached pine and granite. But what was it? The mill, he explained. Todd is the miller, and this is his prized machine, brought all the way from Austria. The wheat kernels, grown up the valley near Armstrong, are poured into the hopper of the mill, then slither

Mill at True Grain Bread
(photo courtesy of the McDonald collection)

down to the granite grinder and emerge at various points along the way, depending on the quality of flour required. As we watched, the mill ground away and the flour slowly sifted out the bottom of one of the hoppers. All of this, in full view of the bakery.

But tasting is the true test so the first task was to order a cinnamon twist and a cup of coffee. Tearing off one oven-warmed layer at a time, inhaling the aroma of cinnamon, munching down the curving arcs of flavour, I was convinced. At least for now.

But what about the breads? Time for the *real* test. Todd explained that every loaf of bread that

is sold today is baked today: yesterday's bread is donated to the local food bank. That policy, combined with their insistence on freshly milled flour, makes for very fresh bread indeed. They bake in small batches and handcraft each loaf. The ingredient list is impressive yet simple: Red Fife sifted wheat, sunflower seeds, sesame seeds, oats, rye, buckwheat, barley, flax, millet, sea salt, filtered water, hazelnuts, and more. In keeping with the German traditions of the Bäckermeister, they offer traditional German rye, an even darker rye studded with pumpkin seeds, a rich Red Fife hazelnut loaf, cracked-grain bread, sourdough bread, and even a large round beauty dedicated to the local landmark—the Giant's Head loaf.

Antoine de Saint-Exupéry was reported to have said that "the flavour of bread shared has no equal," and as I loaded up my shopping bag with treasures, I began to grasp the spirit of the quote. It seems that this is the essence of True Grain Bread, the heart and soul of Summerland. Bread being shared.

———

Most people grow grapes to make wine. A major food group, to be sure. But a select few grow grapes for something else—vinegar. A flavour enhancer that adds acidity to cooking and freshness to salads, vinegar is an important culinary

A selection of products from The Vinegar Works (photo courtesy of the McDonald collection)

ingredient. Tucked away on Gould Avenue behind Summerland, The Vinegar Works is a treasure trove of vinegars. Kim Stansfield and John Gordon have been farming their ten acres of land since the late 1990s, at first with a market garden, then gradually moving into grapes.

They grow Gewürztraminer, Pinot Meunier, and Pinot Noir grapes on two acres of their farm, initially making wine from the grapes and then transforming that wine into flavourful vinegars that reflect the essence of this valley. It might sound less sexy than wine, but a salad of fresh

At Local Lounge and Grille in Summerland

greens dressed with a boutique vinegar—maybe infused with a touch of plum—is like no ordinary salad.

Their Pinot Meunier grapes, which are normally used to make champagne, also produce robust red wine vinegars that taste best when dressing bold Caesar or Greek salads. Another concoction made from the concentrated juices of Pinot Meunier grapes is then added to wine vinegar to make a fine balsamic vinegar. With a hint of sweetness and richness, it is dreamy when drizzled over grilled zucchini, picked fresh from the garden. Gewürztraminer grapes are the source of a subtle white wine vinegar that lightly dresses fresh green salads and, true to the spiciness of the grape, adds a little zest. The Vinegar Works also infuses a selection of vinegars with their homegrown herbs. The tarragon white wine vinegar, not surprisingly, is best combined with chicken. They also grow apricots, plums, raspberries, and elderberries, all of which they use to flavour their Gewürztraminer white wine vinegar.

When I asked Kim about other uses for their vinegars, she directed me to her blogsite, Vinegartart, where she shares recipes that feature their wine vinegars. One dressing, easily made with red wine vinegar, unripened goat cheese, and fresh dill, manages to taste both fresh and unbelievably rich at the same time. Kim's recipes combine their wine vinegars with vegetables fresh from the garden or the farmers' market, depending on the situation. Swiss chard, kale, potatoes, garlic scapes: everything out there in the garden is combined with vinegars and oils and herbs. This blog is worth following for ideas as each new seasonal vegetable presents itself.

If I had only one opportunity to eat a meal in Summerland, it would be at Local Lounge and Grill on Lakeshore Drive. Sited on the shore of Okanagan Lake, the restaurant has two distinct characters: indoors and outdoors. I prefer outdoors. As you lounge on their patio, sailboats moored at the marina next door, the sound of waves lapping up on shore, Local feels very much like the Mediterranean. One of my future plans is to paddle to Local, tie the canoe up at the marina, and wander in for a well-deserved lunch.

Even their hamburgers are amazing. Every element of this homely dish is prepared with care, from the well-seasoned meat to the herb bun to the fresh and crispy fries on the side. The entire menu is seasonal and local and paired with Okanagan wines. Unlike many other fine restaurants in this valley, Local is open all year. Seated by the window on a crisp January day, gazing out at the frost-coated pier and a column of steam rising off the lake, with a bowl of award-winning winter-squash-and-clam chowder, you feel this is just right.

True Grain Bread
10108 Main Street
Summerland, BC

The Vinegar Works
10216 Gould Avenue
Summerland, BC

Local Lounge and Grill
12817 Lakeshore Drive South
Summerland, BC

Views of Dirty Laundry Vineyard

29. Summerland Sips

Summerland is bursting with wineries. Maybe not as many as the Naramata Bench, but quite enough. Most people agree that the very best winery patio in town is up Fiske Street at the Dirty Laundry Vineyard. Spacious, funky, and friendly, this is a great place to unwind after a strenuous bike ride on the Test of Humanity or the historic Kettle Valley Railway, or a swift hike up Giant's Head Mountain. This is a winery with a cheeky sense of humour, as evidenced by the monikers they give their wines, like A Girl in Every Port or Kay-Syrah. Attitude, attitude, attitude.

Where does this sauciness come from? you might ask. It all goes back to the name. In the late nineteenth century, this area was teeming with fur traders, miners, and ranchers. This was also the time when the Canadian Pacific Railway was being built in British Columbia. Over fifteen thousand Chinese labourers toiled away on that project, infamous for its terrible working conditions. One of those Chinese workers fled his job and found his way to the shore of Okanagan Lake at Summerland. Not surprisingly, he opened a Chinese laundry. It did well, but this particular entrepreneur had greater aspirations. He soon realized that other needs were not being met, so he expanded the laundry to include a gambling den and a brothel! Business boomed. Clean clothes *and* satisfied grins!

Although this little piece of Summerland history was not terribly well known, it seemed the appropriate context for the winery and a way to inject some fun into the more serious business of wine. That exuberance is everywhere: on the patio, on the signs, and on the banners surrounding this jaw-droppingly scenic site.

Their merchandising is hilarious: bikini panties with the Dirty Laundry logo and sky-high red heels doubling as bottle holders. The signage is playful, smart, and irreverent. But it's not only about having fun. Dirty Laundry also makes good wine, with names like Naughty Chardonnay, Secret Affair, and Bordello. And although they are not a restaurant, their patio is open to picnics, for which they provide hampers and, during the

Sumac Ridge Estate Winery

summer, a wide array of live music. This place defies you not to smile—at least once.

Nearby, but a tad higher in elevation, is Thornhaven Estates Winery. It, too, boasts a lovely patio. Designed in a Southwestern style, the winery is built on the lower slopes of Little Giant's Head Mountain. It has been in the Fraser family since it opened in 2001. From their airy patio you can see (and hear) the historic Kettle Valley steam train rolling along. Okanagan Lake twinkles in the distance, and the vineyards and orchards of Happy Valley stretch out below.

This is another place to enjoy a picnic, and good wine, particularly the Gewürztraminer, which won the Lieutenant Governor's Award for the 2011 vintage.

A much more upscale ambience is available across the highway and closer to the lake at Bonitas Winery. "A touch of the Mediterranean, Okanagan style," their advertising promises. And it delivers. An elegant and modern structure overlooking neat vineyards cascading down toward the lake, combined with superb wines and even better dining on their sun-drenched patio, makes this a dress-up kind of place.

But the granddaddy of them all is Sumac Ridge Estate Winery, one of the pioneer wineries in the South Okanagan. Its founder, Harry McWaters, is one of the original "characters" in the valley. A true visionary, Harry had to do some serious finagling to get what he wanted: a winery with a licensed restaurant. Back in 1981 this simply wasn't allowed. To solve that problem, he built a small golf course around the structure, allowing him to open a licensed restaurant in his new winery.

Harry managed a number of firsts in the valley: he created the first BC Chardonnay made from estate-grown grapes in 1983; he released the first commercially successful traditional-method sparkling wine in 1989; and he was the first to plant a big vineyard with Bordeaux varietals on Black Sage Road—now famous for its top-quality grapes.

Harry is no longer president of Sumac Ridge. He has gone on to consulting and other challenges, including making his own Harry McWaters Collection of upscale wines from his sixty-acre Sundial Vineyard on the Black Sage Bench.

You probably wouldn't be aware of any of this history from walking into the Sumac Ridge tasting room. Perhaps it doesn't matter. But it's interesting to understand how young the wine industry is in this valley, and how visionary those first wine-makers were. In Okanagan terms, this winery is "historical," imbued with the spirit and vision of Harry McWaters.

Like many other wineries, they make very good wine. My two favourites are their unoaked Chardonnay and their super-oaked Merlot. Chardonnay isn't my favourite white wine. In fact, I tend to avoid it, in part because it is so often heavily oaked. But the unoaked version offered by Sumac Ridge is clean, with a hint of Granny Smith apple and a crisp finish. In dramatic contrast, the Black Sage Vineyard Merlot has so big and rich and fat a taste that you can almost chew the blackcurrant and cherry flavours that ooze from the bottle. This is a wine worth putting down for a few years, but oh, that's so difficult to do.

Patio at Dirty Laundry Vineyard

Dirty Laundry Vineyard
7311 Fiske Sreet
Summerland, BC

Thornhaven Estates Winery
6816 Andrew Avenue
Summerland BC

Bonitas Winery
20623 McDougald Road
Summerland, BC

Sumac Ridge Estate Winery
17403 Highway 97
Summerland, BC

View across Okanagan
Lake from Peachland

30. Peachland Bliss

How important is bread? As has already been established earlier in this volume, it is a fundamental necessity. One of life's basic needs. And when it's delivered with style and grace and nutrition and flavour, what more can a person ask?

What role does a bakery play in a town? Again, it's central to the very core of the community. This is true in Summerland, and it's equally true in Peachland. Bliss Bakery not only produces wonderful bread—my favourite is the sun-dried cranberry sourdough—they also make fabulous sandwiches and soups. Their spicy curry Thai soup is thick and creamy, with the right amount of zing to catch your attention.

The loyalty of Bliss Bakery's customers is legendary. I'm sure it helps that the bakery is situated in a magnificent setting on the shore of Okanagan Lake, looking south all the way to Penticton! Between Bliss Bakery and the lake is an expansive outdoor sitting area, almost always overflowing with people enjoying their coffee and baked goodies, both winter and summer. With its southern exposure and

protective north walls, it's bright and warm here, even in January. At least with a steaming mug of coffee in your hand. Immediately beyond that seating area and a very sleepy road, a walking path extends the entire length of Peachland, a historic and funky town that stretches out along the beach like a string of pearls.

I've been commuting between Banff and Penticton for more than a dozen years and have never, *ever* failed to stop at Bliss Bakery. Although it's conveniently close to Highway 97, it feels an entire world away, quiet and secluded and relaxed. Peachland's Bliss Bakery is now a flagship bakery because Bliss has expanded: a second location opened in Kelowna and a third in Mission.

Wandering along that Peachland pathway, waves crashing up along the shore on stormy winter mornings or lapping like a well-behaved kitten on sun-drenched summer afternoons, is a wonderful way to spend an hour or two. There is absolutely no elevation gain; it's completely flat. So you can run, bike, power walk, stroll,

Bliss Bakery

of the lake, with a patio that's suspended above the water and sailboats moored nearby so there is nothing to separate you from the vast expanse of blue.

But such a strange name—Blind Angler. The story behind the name is a sad one. Jack Wilson settled in Peachland in the early 1900s to log, trap, and grow fruit. Then, while serving in the army during the First World War, he was exposed to mustard gas, which eventually blinded him. But Jack still loved to fish, so fish he did, rowing out from Peachland in his little boat. The Blind Angler Grill honours his memory.

The menu is both inviting and entertaining, with lots of silly little sayings: "People who eat fish are better lovers" and "In spite of the cost of living, it's still popular." The Sunday morning farmers' market, which takes place down the street, provides a steady stream of customers, for both breakfast and lunch. A Blind Angler breakfast favourite is the chorizo hash topped with poached eggs and hollandaise sauce. The Brie-and-pear chicken wrap combines the graininess of pear with the creaminess of Brie and offers up a wonderful mélange of flavours. The hot and spicy calamari is a pleasant, zingy surprise, cooled off with fresh tzatziki. The salmon burger is rich, and even richer when topped with yummy goat cheese. And the cranberry salsa provides the fresh and light balance needed. Ahh, so much choice!

rollerblade—transporting yourself from A to B in all kinds of ways, savouring the views, increasing your heart rate, and potentially enjoying some culinary treats along the way.

One of those treats is near the south end of the Peachland Promenade. Blind Angler Grill, which lies slightly beyond the last marina, looks, feels, and smells like a seaside grill. It's perched on the edge

Peachland Promenade

It's hard to find fault with this place. Friendly. Right on the water. Relaxed. A perfect way to wrap up a morning of wandering along the boardwalk, paddle boarding, or sailing. Lake living at its best. Slow and tasty.

Bliss Bakery
101-4200 Beach Avenue
Peachland, BC

Blind Angler Grill
5899 Beach Avenue
Peachland, BC

Vineyard at Quails' Gate Winery

31. Quails' Gate Winery

My first impression of Quails' Gate Winery was from years ago when my husband and I used to travel from Banff to the Skaha Bluffs to climb. I knew of Quails' Gate because they had been featured at a fundraising dinner at The Banff Centre where I worked. Five courses of fine food carefully paired with Quails' Gate wines. The wines were impressive, so it seemed logical to go the source.

And we did. Turning off the highway at Westbank, we drove up over the hill and down to a modest log cottage that looked more like a backcountry ski cabin than a winery! But this cabin was full of wine. Good wine. I particularly remember the Pinot Noir.

So what is it like now, I wondered, twenty years later? Unbelievable. The Stewart family still owns the place, although it's on to the second generation now. The winery is much, much bigger—on a completely different scale from that quaint log cabin—but the family's goals and values remain the same. The tasting room is huge and the restaurant is grand, but both are designed to complement the pastoral landscape. Nothing jars the senses. The winery is tasteful and elegant in that relaxed Okanagan style. Wood and glass with ivy-draped exterior walls, luscious flower gardens, and flawless views of the lake and the vineyards below.

The Stewarts were actually orchardists before they turned to vines. They grew up on this land, and they appear to respect both the land and the community in which they live. Apart from their obvious focus on wine, their priority is the visitor experience, which makes for a winning formula for anyone who sets foot on this property—even if you don't enter a single building. It's equally pleasant to wander down the grassy promenade between the rows of rose bush–anchored vines to the picnic area at the bottom of the vineyard. The vista out across the lake and up to the winery above is simply superb. Called the Harvest Gathering Site, this open meadow certainly lives up to its name.

Back up at the winery, you can continue wandering around on your own, or perhaps take a tour. There are several choices, everything from a simple

159

Quails' Gate Winery

tour that explains the history of the family and includes visits to the buildings and a tasting, all the way up to more elaborate tours that include food and wine pairings and lectures about wine production. Education is obviously important here.

Old Vines Restaurant is a destination unto itself. Open twelve months of the year, it serves approximately three hundred people per day. Even with that volume, the service manages to be stylish, young, and perky. For starters, the view from the brick patio is world class. Boxwood hedges and roses rim the patio's edge and large umbrellas protect you from the summer sun, while outdoor fireplaces stand by, ready to warm things up in the cool autumn evenings. The clientele varies from boisterous young families to stylish ladies "doing lunch" to biker couples clad in cowboy boots and leather. Everybody has a smile.

Despite the unpretentious ambience, I sense a serious commitment to high-quality food. Coming from prestigious stints in Toronto and Whistler, Executive Chef Roger Sleiman has found his home here at Quails' Gate. His goal, and as he describes it, his privilege, is to showcase the food of the Okanagan. He focuses on local produce, working with farmers from the Osoyoos area early in the season all the way up to those in the North Okanagan as the summer progresses. He personally knows and works with a few top Kelowna farmers and enjoys stomping around the gardens with them, examining and discovering new varieties of tomato and potato and squash. The winery even has its own small garden for a few things that need to be extremely fresh: greens, strawberries, and herbs. His game meats come from Enderby, poultry from the Lower Mainland, and beef from Alberta. Everything else is from the Okanagan.

I asked Chef Sleiman what I should order for lunch.

"Fish or meat?" he asked.

"Hmm, maybe fish?"

"Why don't you let me cook for you," he suggested.

Yes! What followed was heavenly. I wish it could have gone on forever. The salad paired rich red, deep yellow, and bright green heirloom tomatoes with impossibly sweet figs, all resting on a bed of fresh arugula and drizzled with a tart vinaigrette. I dissolved in the tomatoes, assisted in my efforts by a fresh and easy-drinking Chasselas, one of their signature wines, which originated in Switzerland. Next up was a salmon fillet with roasted potatoes seemingly saturated with melted butter and new beans drizzled with an almond sauce, accompanied by a glass of creamy Chardonnay. Would I like dessert? Dear lord, no.

When I asked Chef Sleiman, who is from Lebanon, his thoughts about this valley—his new home—his answer was revealing. "Agriculture defines the Okanagan," he said. Wise words from a chef.

Back in the tasting room I sampled a few more varietals, but my favourite remains the Pinot Noir. This is not too surprising since Quails' Gate is Canada's largest producer of estate-grown Pinot Noir. These grapes now occupy forty acres of the winery's acreage and represent 20 percent of the entire wine production. This winery is clearly committed to Pinot Noir. In fact, winemaker Frank Stanley admits to spending 80 percent of his time thinking about Pinot Noir. I would hate to appear to worship at the altar of Pinot Noir, but even wine critic John Schreiner describes Quails' Gate Pinot Noir as a "seductive wine, beginning with a rush of berry aromas in the glass. The velvet texture adds to the wine's seduction. This is a very elegant wine."[1] I am in complete agreement.

Patio at Quails' Gate

Quails' Gate Winery
3303 Boucherie Road
West Kelowna, BC

Mission Hill Winery

32. The Mission on the Hill

Mission Hill Winery needs to be experienced, even if you have absolutely no interest in wine. The sheer magnitude of owner Anthony von Mandl's vision is astonishing. Born in Vancouver to European parents, he was nurtured on a rich diet of art, music, and sophisticated cuisine. When he realized that wine and food were his true passions, he began to import fine European wines. That led to his dream of establishing a winery in the then relatively unknown Okanagan Valley. But not just any winery. He wanted to create wines that were recognized internationally as some of the very best.

Winemaker John Simes shares that vision. A New Zealand native, Simes learned his craft at the famed Montana winery, where he produced a Sauvignon Blanc that earned him a medal from the prestigious International Wine and Spirit Competition. After a mere two years as winemaker at Mission Hill, Simes won again, with his Chardonnay, making him the only winemaker in the world to win for two different varietals produced half a world apart. When the judges discovered the origin of the wine, they were stunned and insisted on a retasting. The Mission Hill Chardonnay retained its medal.

But even before you get to the wine, there is the dramatic site. As you approach the winery, imposing fortress-like gates give the impression that you are about to enter a very special environment, a sanctuary to the world of wine. Nearly four thousand carefully planted trees and shrubs integrate native species with varietals to enhance the ecological integrity of the grounds.

In order to enter the main winery grounds, you must first pass through a set of contemporary, curved arches held together by a single keystone that was hand chiseled from a five-tonne block of Indiana limestone. Beyond the keystone, a spacious courtyard opens up, in the centre of which stands a striking twelve-storey bell tower. The entire scene is overwhelmingly beautiful, with a terrace, a loggia, a wine education centre, the winery, and an outdoor amphitheatre where everything from Shakespeare to jazz is performed.

Along one side of the courtyard is the Terrace, a classy open-air restaurant with unrestricted views down across Pinot Noir and Chardonnay vineyards to the lake below. They serve light, elegant fare, accompanied by equally delectable Mission Hill wines. At least once in a person's life, the Terrace has to be experienced.

At one end of the Terrace is the estate room, where (by advance arrangement) you can sample from a range of Mission Hill's rarified Estate and Library wines. The room has a double vaulted ceiling and features a number of pieces from the von Mandl family art collection, including a massive Panathenaic amphora that dates back to the Olympics of fourth century BC. Nearby there are seventeenth-century wine bottles rescued from a shipwreck. It is a strange combination of artifacts, but impressive all the same.

Back in the courtyard and farther along the expansive walkway is the loggia, an outdoor room that provides shade without restricting the view. Its simple concrete pillars are capped with a curving roof made of hand-welded sheets of copper. At the far end of the loggia, a small piazzetta overlooks a private garden where a stately Hungarian oak tree lives next to a seventeenth-century Renaissance fountain.

It actually gets better, for next to the bell tower is the wine education centre. Eight-metre-high wooden doors open wide to a museum-style reception hall, known as the Chagall Room. It's called the Chagall Room for a good reason: there, on the featured wall, is *Animal Tales*, a splendid tapestry by Russian-born painter Marc Chagall. The centre does much more than feature artists. A multimedia presentation takes you into the vineyards and explains the grape-growing and winemaking cycle. There is even a teaching kitchen for culinary professionals.

Under all this opulence, cellars have been blasted into volcanic rock. With a capacity of about eight hundred barrels, the cellars provide the climate- and humidity-controlled environment necessary for the fermentation and careful aging of wine. The only source of natural light is from an oculus—a circular, eye-like opening—in one of the walls. The feeling down here is sombre, quiet, almost reverent.

Back out in the courtyard, as you gaze up at the slopes of Mount Boucherie, and across the rolling lawns to the vineyards and the lake below, it's hard to imagine this place not being here. Mission Hill has a timeless quality about it that deserves sufficient time to savour.

Mission Hill Winery
1730 Mission Hill Road
West Kelowna, BC

Still at Okanagan Spirits

33. Kelowna: The Big Apple

Kelowna. The Big Apple. Well—at least the big Okanagan apple. Kelowna is a little bit intimidating. All those high-rises. All that pavement. So many traffic lights. So many Porsches driving around with hockey players at the wheel. How on earth do you connect with the earth, with the water, with the valley, in this metropolis? You have to look a little harder, but you're still probably never more than ten or twenty minutes from something that connects with the soul of this valley.

Ultimately, Kelowna is a city, and a relatively large one at that, at least by Okanagan standards (with a population nudging two hundred thousand). So it's something of a relief to find, smack in the middle of downtown, a boardwalk next to Okanagan Lake. It begins at the William R. Bennett Bridge and continues along the beach, all the way past the yacht cub, the towering hotels, and their luxury boat docks, and into a marshland humming with bird life. With lots of places to sit and enjoy the view along the way, the boardwalk is urban, scenic, and consistently caressed by the fresh lake breeze.

Knox Mountain, which towers at the edge of downtown Kelowna, above the marshland, is one of those volcanic plugs visible up and down the valley. This one has a road right to the top! Certainly you can drive, but many people choose to hike or mountain bike up one of the challenging trails, or run or cycle up the road—the options are endless. A lookout point halfway up provides a panoramic view but is nothing compared to the vista from the very top. Looking south down the lake and across the city, or north up the lake toward Vernon, this view is worth the effort (or non-effort) and gives a sense of the topography of the central Okanagan Valley. It's impossible to grow weary of the views in this valley, and a physical, self-propelled effort to see them makes the reward seem even more special.

───※───

Back in downtown Kelowna, it's a bit overwhelming to try to represent the scope of what is on offer, at least for the palate.

By the marina in downtown Kelowna

RauDZ Regional Table restaurant staunchly supports serving local produce. One of chef Rod Butters's signature dishes showcases chevon (goat) raised at Takoff Farms in Kelowna. The dish includes apricot chutney sausage, masala loin with quinoa and chèvre, and a chai reduction. "The Okanagan really is the chef's ultimate playground," he says, a common mantra of the valley's leading chefs. Butters would know, since he's certainly been around, from the Four Seasons Hotel in Toronto to the Chateau Whistler to Tofino's Wickaninnish Inn. Inducted into the BC Restaurant Hall of Fame in 2007, Butters has been described as a Canadian born, Canadian-trained Canadian chef, the kind who creates what we will eventually call Canadian cuisine. What a concept.

Equally appealing, but in a completely different way, is the Mediterranean Market on Gordon Street. This is my kind of place. An older, unassuming white box of a building perched on a corner in the midst of an old Kelowna neighbourhood, the market is positively humming with activity. I wandered up to the door at about 10:00 AM one weekday morning and paused to admire the mural painted by the door. I mused about how nice and quiet it would be inside, how I would wander around at will, asking all kinds of questions of the idle, slightly bored early-morning staff. Wrong. Wrong. Wrong.

The narrow aisles were thronged with savvy shoppers who clearly knew their way around. I blundered here and there while they patiently gave me some space before zoning in on their favourite pesto sauce, the only vinaigrette worth using, that terribly special oil. And the deli counter? Couldn't get near the place. I could have sworn there was a nationwide run on pastrami. Or provolone. What were all these people doing here? At 10:00 AM? They were ordering their day's worth of cold cuts and cheese, picking up a beautifully constructed and reasonably priced sandwich, scooping up some dark, rich olives. They were stocking their larder with good things to eat. The display above the deli counter was bare bones. No frills. Just meats and cheeses and prices. And I loved the no-nonsense attitude at the checkout counter. Only cash. Simple.

But I walked out empty-handed. I couldn't make a decision with all that pressure!

At least as important as cheese is fish. Codfathers Seafood Market is one of those places where the fish is fresh and varied, and you can find everything from the standard stuff—salmon, oysters, crab, and halibut—to the more exotic— marlin and eel. Jon Crofts and his staff not only sell the fish but also have lots of creative cooking suggestions. His fish, combined with some fresh veggies from the market, a comfortable campsite or a cottage with a kitchen, and a bottle or two of local wine, could be the gateway to heaven. Slow-style heaven.

Back downtown, there are lots of good choices for eating out. The Twisted Tomato has an airy, sunny rooftop dining area with cozy little booths, topped with a pseudo-sunscreen material. It doesn't really work, but it does give a feeling of privacy. Their flatbread smothered with scallops, bacon, sun-dried

RauDZ Regional
Table restaurant

Catch of the day at Codfathers Seafood Market

THE Rotten Grape
FOOD • WINE • FRIENDS

tomatoes, and basil is rich and full of flavour. Even more so is their bruschetta, which is so fresh it fairly explodes in the mouth. It's a fun, relaxed place with a hint of sassiness—as evidenced in the name.

The Rotten Grape is a charming little wine bar tucked into an atmospheric rock-walled cavern on Kelowna's main street.

Their wine list is amazingly inclusive, but this place is not limited to drinking. A tapas atmosphere is the best way to describe what's on offer. Many of the ingredients are from Covert Farms, down the road in Oliver.

Wandering along Bernard Avenue in Kelowna eventually brings you to a window display that can only be described as dazzling: enormous oak barrels on which stand tall, slender bottles in a myriad of shapes that are brimming with clear liquids and decorated with labels that tempt. Names like Poire William, Pinot Noir Grappa, and—best of all—Taboo Absinthe.

And there, in the corner, is an intricate copper distiller, all curves and pipes and dangerous looking. Okanagan Spirits is an intriguing place to pop into to taste something completely different. With products distilled on the premises, as well as at two distilleries in Vernon, this is an internationally acclaimed, award-winning craft distillery. They use only British Columbia fruit and do not use additives, chemicals, or artificial flavours. You can

A selection from Okanagan Spirits

admire the beautiful bottles and the spectacular stills, and even sample the wares. Better yet, since both the Vernon and Kelowna shops are active distilleries, you can take a tour of the actual process and learn how the products are made. It has been called an ice cream shop for adults. In a valley somewhat obsessed with wine, this is a welcome diversion.

Basket Case Picnics is an equally inspired idea, particularly if you have an active day planned. Why waste time swanning around town when you could go for a hike up on Knox Mountain or along the Kettle Valley Railway trestles near Kelowna, or simply saunter along the creek in the Mission Creek Greenway, a 16.5-kilometre corridor that links trails, viewing platforms, and rest spots? A birder's paradise, the greenway is also perfect for running, biking, and horseback riding. But at some point one gets peckish, and that's where Basket Case Picnics steps in. Totally committed to local produce, they can provide a four-course picnic filled with turkey breast, local Brie, peach chutney, carrot cake with lemon cream cheese icing, and more. You can find them at the markets in their mobile truck: in Kelowna on Wednesdays and Saturdays, in Peachland on Sundays, and in Vernon on Mondays and Thursdays. A moveable feast, as Hemingway would say.

RauDZ Regional Table
1560 Water Street
Kelowna, BC

Mediterranean Market
1570 Gordon Drive
Kelowna, BC

Codfathers Seafood Market
2355 Gordon Drive
Kelowna, BC

Twisted Tomato
371 Bernard Avenue
Kelowna, BC

The Rotten Grape
231 Bernard Avenue
Kelowna, BC

Okanagan Spirits
267 Bernard Avenue, Kelowna, BC
and 2920 28th Avenue, Vernon, BC

Basket Case Picnics
2405 Taylor Crescent
Kelowna, BC

Summerhill Pyramid Winery

34. Kelowna Wine

In such a busy community it can be difficult to find those out-of-the-way places that are charming, authentic, and local. But they do exist. One of the more unusual destinations is Summerhill Pyramid Winery on Chute Lake Road, the route that eventually leads to Kelowna's rock-climbing area, Kelowna Crags. Summerhill is a completely organic winery, an experiment that appears to be working. Even famed artist Robert Bateman agrees, since he's allowing prints of his artwork to grace their labels.

Despite its twenty-year history in the valley, Summerhill seems slightly futuristic (or ancient, depending how you look at it). Its signature pyramid structure dominates the landscape when you first spy it, but it is not meant to shock. In fact, the pyramid is an integral part of the winemaking vision of owner Stephen Cipes. A combination of big city businessman and New Age mystic, Cipes doesn't mince words: "We have a twenty-year experiment proving the effect of sacred geometry on liquids with a twenty-year track record of international gold medals." His goal has always been to make the finest wines in the world, especially sparkling wines. The French place their sparkling wines in a cool dark place for thirty days and that's what Cipes does too—under the pyramid! His wines are made of 100 percent organically grown grapes using a minimal-intervention winemaking process. The clarification process in the pyramid is the final step and the results are impressive. His sparkling wines erupt in bubbles and flavour. They win prizes—even in France—against their French competition!

But there's more to the pyramid than making wine. Cipes encourages visitors to the winery to turn off their cellphones and take a few moments from their busy lives to simply *be* inside the pyramid. No talking. Just standing or sitting on the floor, and breathing. He explains that the word *pyr-a-mid* means "fire in the middle," and goes on to suggest that we all have fire in our middle: it is our heart and our soul. Furthermore, he insists, if wine can be clarified by the pyramid, it should be possible for humans, who are mostly liquid, to be clarified too. It's certainly worth a try. And even if clarification isn't achieved, quiet and peace and reflection are—a good way to spend some slow time.

Behind the pyramid lies an unusual juxtaposition of Okanagan history. A young Englishman, Henry Cecil Mallam, arrived here in 1904 and settled into a classy two-storey, hand-hewn log house. Mallam brought over his library, good furniture, and precious tea sets, and soon found himself a wife. Near the Mallam house is an authentic *kekuli*. This inspiring natural structure of earth and logs was built by members of the Westbank First Nation and is a re-creation of the traditional winter home of Kelowna's First People. Both the Mallam house and the kekuli are open to the public, and for bird lovers, there is a modest little bird sanctuary on the property. They have a restaurant as well, the Sunset Organic Bistro, which is best enjoyed at sunset.

Summerhill also has a close alliance with the arts and science. The winery has played host to sultry singers, Tibetan gongs, musical theatre, dinner with David Suzuki, jazz ballet, a pyramid healing concert, and even a fertility festival.

Summerhill Pyramid Winery deserves some time: time to understand the history; time to experience the pyramid magic; and time to enjoy a tasting and, finally, a relaxing late-afternoon tapas or dinner, watching that deep-orange Okanagan sun slide below the horizon.

The southeast corner of Kelowna provides probably the best example of old-style Okanagan agriculture. Farmers have been growing fruit and vegetables here for decades. In recent years some of those crops have been transformed into vineyards. But not all. The area is a healthy mix of organic farms, aviaries, lavender farms, and—yes—wineries. My favourite is Tantalus Vineyards. Easily reached from downtown Kelowna in ten minutes by car or twenty minutes on a bike (better—because it makes it easier to access all the other interesting things around here), Tantalus is a strange and wonderful mix of old and new, sophisticated and simple, urban and country.

Let's start with the entrance. The slightly uneven grey, dusty gravel road that leads down from Dehart Road is highly unusual for a winery—at least one of this significance. No pavement. No smelly tar. Just gravel. It screams "country." Next is the building. The LEED-certified winery is stark, functional, and surprisingly elegant. In front of the extremely simple building is a vegetable garden. Another good sign.

Inside the building, there is a feeling of vast open space. At one end of the "great room," you can peer into the barrel room, and beyond, into the actual winery. On the other side of the soaring windows are the vineyards themselves. And at the opposite end of the room, in the remarkably modest tasting area, are the bottles of finished wine. From field to table. From vineyard to bottle. It's all visible, in one sweeping glance.

Despite the simplicity of the place, there are some distractions. The walls are covered in superb pieces of art: Takao Tanabe banners, Edward Burtynsky photographs, and Dempsey Bob masks. Artfully and subtly lit, the masks seem to float on the wall, watching, observing. Is this a gallery or a winery?

The staff explains: First and foremost it's a winery. But as fortune would have it, the owner is a serious art collector and has chosen to share his collection with those who come into this space. The artwork changes frequently and curators from other galleries are invited to bring exhibitions of serious art to the winery as well.

Across from the magnificent pieces is an entire wall of glass. A really *big* wall. Not just a wall of windows, it is a series of massive sliding-glass panels. With the wonderful view of the vineyards below, a cozy fireplace in the corner, and oodles of space, it's a mystery what this room was actually designed for, since the tastings take place down at the end. The staff explains that this is where Tantalus dinners and gatherings take place. The glass panels disappear into the walls to create a gigantic space that embraces indoors and outdoors. Seamless. I decide then and there that I want to be at one of those dinners.

Everything at Tantalus starts in the vineyard. Naturally all the best winemakers in the valley say this, so what makes this place special? The Tantalus story emerges: The original forty-eight acres of this vineyard were first farmed in 1927 by the Hughes family. Martin Dulik bought it in 1932 and planted some vines. 1932! That makes it one of the (if not *the*) oldest continuous vineyard in the Okanagan Valley. Martin started with table grapes, moved to hybrids, and finally settled on vinifera grapes. The property changed hands again in the 1970s, but Martin's son, Dan Dulik, still works in the vineyard.

This brings up an interesting point, for when you look at photos of the Tantalus vineyards, you can't help but notice a lot of elderly gentlemen working with the vines. This too has a story. As the current owner gradually acquired property from southeast Kelowna farmers, many of them took advantage of the homesite severance option, which allows them to continue living in their original homes in this rural paradise. But what to do? Suddenly they were cash rich but with too much time on their hands. Many of them chose to work in the vineyards, to continue a life of growing things. That's the "old" part of this winery, along with many of the Riesling vines.

What's new? The winemaking team, for one. Led by David Paterson, the youngsters decided in

Tantalus Vineyards

Chardonnay. That's it. Paterson admits to currently being "in love" with Block 5 of the Old Riesling vineyard. That means he creates that particular Old Vines Riesling with extra care and attention.

Tantalus also understands economy of scale. Since acquiring the land they have expanded from forty-eight to seventy-five acres, and it's not over yet. But, quite unusual for a winery, all the land is contiguous. They don't have vineyards in Osoyoos. They don't have vineyards across the lake. They only have vineyards that connect with the original forty-eight acres, and that's all they're interested in farming.

Wine is important, but so is stewardship. Stewardship of this agricultural community that has been farming here since the 1920s. Stewardship of the land. Not only for agricultural purposes, but also for environmental ideals. Tantalus farms naturally. Not organically, but as naturally as possible and with as much ecological diversity as possible.

There are forty-two beehives on the property, in support of Arlo's Honey Farm up the road. They own a ten-acre forest located between two of their vineyards that houses raptors and coyotes. There are nesting boxes all over the place, many for bluebirds. Owls and hawks and golden eagles are visible from those magnificent sliding doors. Tantalus is in the middle of one of the oldest agricultural areas of the entire Okanagan Valley, yet

2004 that Tantalus would be special. Every single block of vines in the vineyards has a different aspect and is specifically delineated. Each is treated differently, harvested at a different time, and blended with care and intelligence into the few specialty wines that Tantalus offers. The winemaking team understands every bit of this terroir and they produce wines accordingly: Riesling, Pinot Noir, and

they still make space for birds and mammals and insects and gardens.

But ultimately, Tantalus is about fabulous wine. The Riesling is rich and inviting, with some lovely hints of lime and grapefruit, but back one level there is a minerality that seems to focus it, laserlike, to a clean finish. I could drink this wine every single day. Anthony Gismondi described it in the *Vancouver Sun* as "pure, electric mineral floral citrus green apple fruit without any overpowering sulphur . . . the attack is textbook crisp and clean."[1] Even British wine guru and *Oxford Companion to Wine* author Jancis Robinson raves, rating the 2008 Old Vines Riesling the top white Canadian wine. The Pinot Noir is in a class of its own. Its deep maroon colour suggests brown sugar and Bing cherries. It's earthy and full of those dark Okanagan fruits: plum and red rhubarb and raspberry. It's velvety and elegant, and I am hard pressed to put this wine down for a couple of years, which I know I must do in order to experience its fullness.

The hand weeding, the deficit watering, the careful soil preparation, and the use of organic composting pay off. These wines are special. This place is special. There is almost nothing, other than wine, to buy in this gorgeous, simple room. There is only the view, the barrel room, the wonderful art, and the wine. Oh yes, the wine. How big is the trunk in my car?

Apiary at Tantalus Vineyards

Summerhill Pyramid Winery
4870 Chute Lake Road
Kelowna, BC

Tantalus Vineyards
1670 Dehart Road
Kelowna, BC

Myra Canyon trestles (photo courtesy of the McDonald collection)

35. Myra Canyon

The morning mist clung like netting to the forest of black stumps. It was early, not yet 8:00 AM, and cool for a July morning. Not another soul was at the trailhead. It felt kind of strange: we were the only ones here in this massive parking lot, quietly unloading our bikes, grabbing a quick sip of coffee from the thermos before heading up the trail. We were about to enter what is essentially a living outdoor museum: the Myra Canyon section of the Kettle Valley Railway outside Kelowna.

At the turn of the twentieth century, a mining boom flashed through the East and West Kootenays: gold, silver, zinc, and copper were all found. In order to distribute the minerals, a railway link was needed between the Kootenay riches and the ports of Vancouver and New Westminster. The Kettle River Valley Railway was the solution. Construction, which began in 1910, faced two major hurdles: the Coquihalla Canyon near Hope, and the Okanagan Highland, which separated the Kootenays from the Okanagan Valley and contained a series of plunging canyons. Since the railway was expected to have a maximum grade of 2.2 percent, the Okanagan section required a series of long switchbacks east of Penticton, up to Chute Lake Pass and the Myra Canyon trestles high above Kelowna.

Myra Canyon is an impressive gorge: deep, steep, and wide, with two main creeks—the East Canyon and West Canyon creeks. The convoluted wrinkles of this tortured landscape demanded eleven kilometres of track and twenty wooden trestles. All of this to make a mere one and a half kilometres of headway and span the gaping chasms of the canyon. It wasn't until 1914 that the Myra Canyon section was finally completed.

Thanks to the completion of the KVR, British Columbia's southern interior thrived for the next sixty years. But all good things come to an end: the Midway-to-Penticton section of the KVR—including Myra Canyon—carried its last train in 1972. Eight years later the rails were removed and the provincial government acquired the right-of-way. Initially, the trail and the trestles fell into disrepair from vandalism and neglect. But people

Airy trestles
(photo courtesy of the
McDonald collection)

still used the trail. They couldn't help themselves. It was such a dramatic landscape. Twenty years later the Myra Canyon Trestle Restoration Society was formed, with the object of restoring the trestles to make them safer for the public.

Over the next few seasons, a volunteer army decked each trestle with four-foot boardwalks and equipped them with guardrails. The tunnels were all rescaled. These efforts began to produce results, for visitation increased to the point that they had to install pit toilets. The Myra Canyon section of the KVR had become famous: visitor numbers eventually climbed to fifty thousand people per season.

Then came the devastating fire of 2003. Over two hundred Kelowna homes were destroyed, as well as more than twenty thousand acres of forest and parkland. In September of that year, the wildfire reached the Myra Canyon trestles and people watched in horror and disbelief as it destroyed twelve of the sixteen wooden structures and critically damaged the two steel bridges.

Again, volunteers rallied to the task. The first trestle, Number 18, was rebuilt in the fall of 2004, just one year after the fire. Three and a half years later the restoration was complete.

You can feel this history and sense the repeated Herculean efforts as you ride the Myra

Canyon trail. The rock walls and rock slides are still scorched black as coal from the fire, and the surrounding hills are a pincushion of blackened stumps. It's impossible not to be subdued by this violent act of nature, yet, at the same time, it's equally difficult not to marvel at the turn-of-the-century construction feats that surmounted the many drainages. When this section of trail was first constructed, the equipment used was pretty elementary: horses, mules, steam shovels, black powder, hand tools, and manual labour. And because the terrain wasn't flat, but rather rose and fell, the design of the trestles was complex. Again, the tools used were from a different era: trigonometric tables, logarithmic tables, Smoley's tables of slopes and rises, and slide rules.

Despite the dramatic scenery and the history, the trail is user-friendly. It's double track the entire way, and the bridges' sturdy railings make it almost impossible for a cyclist to catapult into the abyss. And despite the challenges, the grade remains at around 2.2 percent. The distance from Myra Station to Ruth Station is about nine kilometres one way, with an elevation gain of one hundred and fifty metres. As you pedal along, staring at the unfolding scenery and the gaping void beneath your legs, you hardly notice the fact that you are indeed going up, ever so gently. Turning around at Ruth Station and returning along the same trail is an easy cruise, proof of the elevation gain.

Although not blessed with as spectacular of views as from the KVR above the Naramata Bench, and not as directly connected to the old train that still runs in Summerland, this section of the historic railway is special in different ways. It is a remnant of another era in this valley—an era of gold and riches and entrepreneurs, and skilled workers helping to make the impossible possible.

It was late morning by the time we had cycled the route from Myra Canyon to Ruth Station and back. The mist had been burned off by the morning sun. As we rolled into the parking lot after our solitary ride, we were shocked to see dozens of people: reading the signs, unloading bikes, even renting bikes at a rental trailer that had miraculously appeared. It was gratifying to see all this enthusiasm for such a significant stretch of trail. But secretly I was glad we had risen early that day.

Myra Canyon Trestles ride
Head north on Highway 97 through the city of Kelowna, and turn right on Pandosy Road. Follow Pandosy for 3.5 km, and turn left onto KLO Road. After 8.7 km turn right on McCulloch Road. McCulloch becomes a gravel road at 14.5 km. Turn right, going uphill, at 16.7 km, and gain elevation (350 m) until you reach the old remnants of Myra Station at 25.5 km. Turn right into the parking lot. Cycling the trestle section of the KVR takes an easy half day.

Barrel room at Ex Nihilo Vineyards

36. Lake Country

On the back road between Kelowna and Vernon lies an idyllic stretch of country. With Okanagan Lake anchoring the landscape below, the hills fold and bend with increasing lushness as you make your way north. The changes are subtle but they're there. Very little sagebrush and rabbit brush, more Douglas fir to complement the ponderosa pine forest, less open grassland and more consistent forest cover. The air has a wee bit more humidity, and the sun is not quite as intense. As you begin to approach the northern reaches of this valley, the desert influences of the south slowly lose their grip. The Lake Country route winds through vineyards, orchards, and forests, offering up a new view at every turn. A veritable "slow road," well away from the main Highway 97, it is best biked, as there's very little traffic.

Not surprisingly, there are wineries. Not nearly as many as down south, but a few. And at least one of them has been here for a very long time—more than thirty years. Gray Monk Estate Winery has always occupied the same position on the east bank of Okanagan Lake in Lake Country, but its look has changed dramatically. Once a quaint little place, Gray Monk has matured and grown. Its new wine shop is almost three times as big as before, and the new restaurant is spacious and affords a truly stunning view. Although Gray Monk gets many of its grapes from farther south in the valley, some of its signature wines are made from grapes grown right on site. And those are the ones that I think represent Gray Monk best: varietals such as Pinot Auxerrois, Ehrenfelser, and Siegerrebe, a favourite of owner Trudy Heiss.

A nearby winery with a completely different style is Ex Nihilo Vineyards. Famous for its connection to the Rolling Stones and its wild, fly-in-from-LA parties, Ex Nihilo has a reputation to live up to. "Out of nothing" is exactly what the pioneers of this winery had in mind when they first saw the empty ten-acre parcel of steep, southwest-facing property.

A marketing partnership with the Rolling Stones certainly hasn't hurt business. Their wines

183

**Ex Nihilo's flagship
Rolling Stones ice wine**

are, by most accounts, expensive: the Riesling is good value for its price, but their Merlot comes at a substantial bump in cost, the Meritage blend—called Satisfaction—slightly higher still, and the coup de grace—the Sympathy for the Devil icewines—comes in at well over a hundred dollars per *half* bottle.

It's not only the Rolling Stones connection and the price tags that impart a feeling of boldness. You can feel it as soon as you roll into the parking lot. Ahead is a sprawling terracotta winery topped with a black tile roof, basking in the sunshine amid generous lawns. The dramatic barrel room is punctuated with bold fixtures and abstract paintings. Spectacular Art Deco light fixtures compete with the soaring views. And the in-your-face extended tongue on the Sympathy for the Devil icewine bottles reveals not one hint of bashfulness.

At some point, everyone needs to eat—a proper meal at a proper restaurant. Luckily, a solution awaits! Ricardo's Mediterranean Kitchen. It's not that easy to find, and when you do actually find it, the location probably wouldn't be described as ideal. In fact, this place reminds me of times I've spent in the Liguria area of Italy, travelling with the locals, rock climbing during the day, and eating well in the evenings, often at out-of-the-way places that don't look like much until you get inside, smell the aromas, hear the lilting sounds of the Italian language, and feel the warm welcome. That is the feeling at Ricardo's. There is something so *Italian* about this place.

Located in the tiny village of Winfield, the restaurant is at the end of a road, tucked up against the train tracks, *inside* a trailer park. A simple white building with a bold, bigger-than-life sign that reads RICARDO'S MEDITERRANEAN KITCHEN! Sound inviting? Okay, maybe not. But wait, take another look. The walled garden is stuffed with comfy furniture, outrageous sculptures, funky paintings, and a gurgling fountain to finish things off. Live jazz throbs late into the night every Thursday, and famous chef Ricardo Scebba dishes up his scrumptious family recipes, often with his mother, Concetta, at his side.

Ricardo buys his vegetables from nearby Lake Country Culinary Farms and pairs his dishes with Lake Country wines. What's his most successful dish? I ask. Nothing Italian, it turns out. Blackened prime ribs. Darn, that's not what I wanted to hear. What about his most popular Italian dish? Spaghetti and meatballs. Okay, that's better.

His counter overflows with rows of awards and his cookbook, *That's Amore*, is a bestseller. His sense of humour informs every recipe. When asking for one cup or more of extra-virgin olive oil for his

Ricardo's in Winfield
(photo courtesy of the McDonald collection)

"mother sauce," he adds, "This is not a typo." He includes a disclaimer with his Greek ribs recipe: "I'm not just some over-confident Italian who thinks he knows how to cook Greek food." He learned to cook from his mother and grandmother and dedicated the cookbook to Concetta.

A local cookbook, using local foods, paired with local wines and filled with amusing and poignant local stories—it all fits. This out-of-the-way place is an Okanagan gem and well worth searching out.

Gray Monk Estate Winery
1055 Camp Road
Lake Country, BC

Ex Nihilo Vineyards
1525 Camp Road
Lake Country, BC

Ricardo's Mediterranean Kitchen
415 Commonwealth Road
Winfield, BC

Strawberry abundance at the Vernon Farmers' Market
(photo courtesy of the McDonald collection)

37. Vernon's German Heritage

Vernon has a slightly more sedate feel than its cousins, Kelowna and Penticton, to the south. Snuggled in among Okanagan, Kalamalka, and Swan Lakes, it feels protected by the forested hills above. Vernon is also a hotbed of sausage. In fact, at one time the highest concentration of sausage makers in North America was in the North Okanagan, probably because of the many German immigrants in this area.

One of the very best places for sausage is Ritter's European House of Sausage. Otto Ritter is a fourth-generation sausage maker and was a kid when his family came from Germany to the North Okanagan, intending to buy a butcher shop south of town. When they arrived they were shocked to learn that the shop had already been sold. They stayed anyway, and now supply sausages to a steady stream of loyal customers. I could see (and taste) why. Their pepperoni sausage is dry, spicy, and absolutely delightful. Ideal for a picnic or a hike. As Otto described the attributes and characteristics of each and every sausage on display, he insisted that his wildly popular smokies are best prepared steamed, since this method preserves the flavour. (To be honest, I prefer to barbecue them, but I would never tell Otto.)

Helmut's Sausage Kitchen is another of those marvellous sausage places. And this place is *huge*. Forty years ago, Helmut's parents launched H&P Sausage Kitchen, a shop that became a standby for anyone wanting locally made sausage. When they retired, Helmut opened his own place, a brand new facility where the sausages are made in the kitchen and sold in the adjoining brightly lit, spacious showroom. You can even watch the process via a video feed from the kitchen to the shop. Helmut has opened a second shop in Kelowna, so successful has he been in Vernon.

The sausages—and all the meat products at Helmut's—are divine. And there are so many kinds: Mennonite farmer's sausage, soppressata salami, beer sausage, Italian sausage, Bavarian meat loaf, Cornish pasties, and more. My favourite might be the double-smoked Italian sausage.

Helmut's Sausage Kitchen

But maybe not. Their prosciutto Westphalia is also incredibly tasty, so thinly sliced, with just enough moisture to keep it all together.

Apart from the fantastic quality of their meats, what struck me upon visiting Helmut's was the infectious enthusiasm of the staff, and the obvious community that existed among the patrons. They all seemed to know each other, chatting about this and that while selecting their day's sausages with care. And yes, most of them were German.

But not everyone eats meat. Luckily for Vernon, there is a "northern" branch of the Mediterranean Market, which, unlike its southern mate in Kelowna, is a spacious store. Packed full of goodies, it has every possible kind of cheese, salami, olive oil, vinegar, mustard, pasta, or flour that you could imagine. The proprietors, David and Bonnie Schwab, understand the cultural diversity of this community and have responded accordingly. They import products for the Dutch market, the German market, the Portuguese, Indian, Greek, French, Polish, Swiss, Croatian, Norwegian markets—you name it, they have it. The cheese display almost makes one weep. Stacks of free-run eggs, and, as in Kelowna, their wonderfully wholesome and appetizing sandwiches. Perfect to take on a hike or bike ride.

And in keeping with the German tradition, one of the very best bakeries in Vernon is the Okanagan Bake House. A German bakery, it is owned by Mechtild Wirtz. Although not the easiest place to find, and easy to miss because it doesn't scream "bakery," it's worth the search. The shelves heave with dark, heavy loaves, shaped with love, baked with respect, and to be eaten with gusto.

The Vernon Farmers' Market, held each Thursday morning in the parking lot at the arena, reflects the products of the North Okanagan. Zelaney Farms based in Lavington is a fantastic source of vegetables. Eagle Rock Road near Armstrong is well represented with half a dozen strawberry farms. Triple Island Farm in Lumby makes Emmental, Gouda, and other hard cheeses. Like all the farmers' markets in the valley, the Vernon market is a living example of field to table that changes with the seasons.

Ritter's European House of Sausage
4305 31st Street
Vernon, BC

Helmut's Sausage Kitchen
2103 48th Avenue
Vernon, BC

Mediterranean Market
500-3115 48th Avenue
Vernon, BC

Okanagan Bake House
Suite 1, 1800 Kalamalka Lake Road
Vernon, BC

Kalamalka Lake

38. Cosens Bay to Coldstream

Of all the bodies of water in this valley, Kalamalka Lake is the jewel in the crown. It's all about the colour. Or in this case, colours. Jade green, indigo blue, cerulean, turquoise, charcoal grey: any and all of these hues might appear on a single day, depending on the angle of the sun, the depth of the lake, and the amount of calcium carbonate deposit in that particular part of the lake. Kalamalka Lake Provincial Park, which is next to the lake, is laced with hiking and biking trails and endowed with tiny, immaculate beaches.

The secluded Cliff Beach and Cosens Bay Beach are two of the best in the entire Okanagan, ideal for swimming or paddle boarding, or simply appreciating the beauty of this very special lake. There's even rock climbing! On the east side of the lake, and still part of the park, is the Cougar Canyon rock-climbing area with over two hundred climbs in eight sectors. The rock is that gorgeous, edgy, climber-friendly gneiss found up and down the valley.

Adjacent to Kalamalka Lake, although not in the Okanagan Valley proper, is the Coldstream Valley. Famous for its extensive, historic, and still-operational Coldstream Ranch, this valley is special because it is the gateway to *real* mountains. From here, among the enormous herds of cattle roaming the Coldstream Ranch pastures, you can see snow all year long, as the Monashee Mountains glimmer in the distance at the head of the valley.

Partway up the valley is the community of Lavington, where orchards and small ranches are the norm. And there, on the side of the easily biked Kalamalka Road, is Countrytyme Gardens, a relaxing place to eat and spend the morning, surrounded by flowers and gardens and orchards.

The morning is probably what it'll take, because the whole world seems to have discovered this place, despite its relatively remote location. The Friesen family, owners of Countrytyme Gardens, has planted a market garden out back with tomatoes, peppers, strawberries, raspberries, and fruit trees, all of which provide the ingredients for what they cook, bake, and sell out front. Their

The Countrytyme garden

Patio at Countrytyme Gardens

cinnamon buns are legendary, but the hearty beet borscht and jams and pies are equally mouth-watering. They even make their own ketchup! All of their pasta sauces are made from their own ingredients and their bread is home-baked. The eggs? From the chickens out back.

Friesen's Countrytyme Gardens
9172 Kalamalka Road
Coldstream, BC

Davison Orchards Country Village

39. Davison Orchards and Honey

On the other side of the valley, snaking high above the eastern arm of Okanagan Lake, is a winding scenic route, Bella Vista Road. And just above the road is a very special, tucked-away attraction: Davison Orchards Country Village.

There are a lot of things going on here, but I'll begin (and probably conclude) with my favourite—the pie. There is nothing quite like a fruit pie made with fruit that has never seen the inside of a motorized vehicle. Auntie May's pies are stupendous creations of flavour and juice and flaky crust, and they are made on site with fruit grown in these very orchards.

But not everybody eats pie. Some prefer vegetables. The farm has fifty acres of orchards and vegetable gardens from which produce is picked daily for their market. This is like a farmers' market one-stop shop. Brilliant green and red peppers, enormous pumpkins, gnarly, knobby squash, a bewildering assortment of apples (twenty-one varieties), corn, berries, and garlic. It's all here and it's all local.

There's more. Apple juice, jams and jellies, apple butter syrup, relishes, and pumpkin butter—the imagination and productivity of this place boggles the mind. They seem to have thought of everyone. They have antique tractors and a petting zoo, a shop bulging with tempting goods, and Auntie May's Deep Dish Café where—you guessed it—they serve Auntie May's pies!

Abundance!

On the way back to town, there is a rather unusual spot. At the Planet Bee Honey Farm and Meadery, you can watch hundreds of honeybees bustling about behind glass, producing their varied and healthy products: bee pollen used to treat hay fever and other allergic reactions, honey used as a natural alternative to processed sugar, and many more.

Orchards, gardens, flowers, bees, and pie—an unbroken circle of productivity.

Planet Bee meadery

Davison Orchards Country Village
3111 Davison Road
Vernon, BC

Planet Bee Honey Farm and Meadery
5011 Bella Vista Road
Vernon, BC

Watermelons a go-go at Davison Orchards!

The Village
Cheese Company

40. Armstrong and the Far North

Armstrong is a funky little town, split in two by the railroad. This intrusion used to be a major drag, but the town fathers have taken a sow's ear and made a silk purse out of it, landscaping along the tracks, creating a one-way road system, and restoring the town's historic buildings. The end result is a charming main street in a town that is surrounded by oat fields, wheat fields, grassy pastures, goat farms, pig farms, dairies, and raspberry and strawberry farms.

Possibly best known for the Armstrong Fair, which has been plugging along for over one hundred years, this little town has a lot more than a fair going for it. Smack in the middle of the North Okanagan agricultural district, Armstrong is the land of milk, cheese, grains, and berries. It shouldn't be a surprise, then, that you can find friendly family restaurants serving good, homemade food made from lots of fresh-from-the-farm ingredients.

The Brown Derby is one of those places, a modest little café with a not-so-modest tagline,

"The world's best breakfast." Judging by the crowds, they might be right. Maybe not in the *world*, but at least in the North Okanagan. The owners, who came to Armstrong from Darlington, England, seem to know what constitutes a good breakfast. Maybe it's all those years of eating the "full English breakfast" that prepared them for Armstrong.

Away from the centre of town and closer to Highway 97 is The Village Cheese Company. It was started by two guys who used to work at the massive Armstrong Cheese company before it moved north and east to Edmonton. Instead of sticking with the company, they decided to stay in Armstrong and create a boutique version of Armstrong Cheese.

Like a good winery, Village Cheese believes that top-quality products start in the field—in this case the pasture—with hand-picked cows bred for high-quality milk and fed with the lushest grasses in the Okanagan Valley. Cheese is simply

The Brown Derby Café, complete with host

concentrated milk, so starting with the best milk probably sets the stage for superior cheese. Field to table once again.

Since this is an artisan fromagerie, everything is done by hand: warming the fresh milk with natural cultures and kosher-approved rennet, cutting the curd and turning it to remove the whey, and, finally, filling the hoops that shape the cheese. The extra work pays off, for their cheeses are excellent. One of my favourites is their smoked-salmon cheese. Strange combination? Perhaps, but try it. Divine.

Between Armstrong and Vernon on Larkin Cross Road stands a set of industrial-looking buildings and equipment—tall granaries, cranes, sheds, and trucks, completely surrounded by grain fields. This is the home of Rogers Foods. I used to come here years ago when our family first moved to Vernon, to buy flour and bran and the other baking ingredients my mother used on a regular basis. It seemed a quaint place in the country.

When I returned, more than thirty years later, it was immediately after a trip to Saskatchewan. There, on the prairies, I had seen endless fields of wheat, oats, and barley ripening in the hot summer sun, so heavy with grains that the stalks could no longer support the weight. A bumper

Downtown Armstrong

crop, the farmers said. A beautiful sight, and one I didn't expect to see again for some time. Imagine my delight when, upon driving into the flat, featureless parking lot at Rogers Foods, I saw, straight ahead, a field of grain ripening in the hot summer sun. Not only was there grain, but a combine was harvesting that grain. For Rogers Foods. Field to table. It's a common mantra of Slow Food. The grain that was growing and being harvested at the very edge of the parking lot would go directly into those massive bins and then into the mill. Some of it would end up in the Rogers Bulk Food Store. Much more would end up in the far corners of the world.

Before I entered the store, a photographic display and some relics of old machines caught my eye. The story began in 1951 when a Seventh Day Adventist couple, Alfred and Pauline Rogers, set up a stone mill to grind flour and cereal for their family. It wasn't long before neighbours began

The "great divide"

popping in, and the Rogers were soon supplying quality flour and cereal products to the entire community.

The next generation brought the enterprise to another level in the early 1970s, when Stan, the son, joined the company. With some major modernization modifications, Rogers began supplying flour products to British Columbia grocery stores and bakeries. The business was bought in 1989 by an international company, Nisshin Seifun, Japan's largest flour-milling company. A new state-of-the art plant was built in 1996, and then something peculiar happened. Four years later the mill went organic. After lots of red tape and changes in production methodology, Rogers is now a certified organic mill, providing products to stores around the world. Yet, somehow, it has retained its small-town, neighbourly feel.

fromageries like Poplar Grove, all the way down on the Naramata Bench. This land grows the best raspberries and strawberries in the entire valley, filling the farmers' markets and providing those precious and intense flavours that vinegar specialists and distilleries use to infuse their products with that special bit of Okanagan freshness.

The Okanagan Valley is not terribly long or wide. But it is amazingly varied, and it is equally productive. From the southern deserts to the northern lushness, it keeps on giving, albeit at a slow pace. Whether you like paddling on a lake, searching for a bird, crunching down on a crisp apple, or sipping a superb Syrah, this valley has something to offer.

This is the North Okanagan, near the "great divide"; the Okanagan River flows south and everything north of it is in the Shuswap River system. It is an area that capitalizes on a climate and soil type that supports the grain crops that supply not only Rogers Foods, but bakeries to the south, like True Grain in Summerland. The land supports dairies that provide milk, not only for Armstrong's Village Cheese Company, but also for

The Brown Derby Café
3425 Pleasant Valley Road
Armstrong, BC

The Village Cheese Company
3475 Smith Drive
Armstrong, BC

Rogers Foods Ltd.
4420 Larkin Cross Road
Armstrong, BC

Skiing at Sovereign Lake (photo courtesy of the McDonald collection)

41. Snowy Conclusion

Although I didn't know it at the time, I started up this slow road more than forty-five years ago when I first arrived in the North Okanagan on that snowy December night. But you and I, and my partner in this book, artist Karolina Born-Tschümperlin, began our journey together in the south, slowly working our way north past lakes and streams, up dry stony trails, and into some of the lesser-known corners of the valley.

We tasted some incredibly juicy cherries in our travels. We made salads from lettuce picked fresh that morning. We treated ourselves to some gourmet meals, accompanied by the best wines in the country. We earned those meals, because we hiked the trails and biked the back roads, paddled the lakes, and tested our skill on the vertical cliffs of Skaha.

Along the way we learned about the flora and fauna of this unique Canadian valley. We discovered the spots where rattlers like to snooze. We scouted out the best places to see a white-throated swift careening through the air. We now know when to look for balsamroot blooms and when to search for the mariposa lily. We stuffed our noses into lavender bunches until we sneezed. And we filled our eyes, over and over, with the beauty of the landscape.

This has taken time. Seasons worth of time. Our experiences in this valley have progressed from those first spring blossoms to the celebration of the fall wine harvest.

But winter also has its charm. And in the Okanagan Valley, one of the most appealing gems for a slow traveller in winter is up in the north, at the Sovereign Lake cross-country ski area.

Sovereign Lakes is the place where World Cup racers and nonagenarians can ski together. Fifty kilometres of trails, combined with an equally large area in adjoining Silver Star Provincial Park, have resulted in a world-class Nordic skiing paradise. The trails are well designed, with everything from gently undulating novice tracks to squirrelly corkscrew advanced runs that keep you focused and over your skis. One of my favourites is the Lars Taylor trail, which climbs to the very top of the

mountain and rewards you with a fast run down. I've done it dozens of times with my brothers and father, always marvelling that this ninety-plus gentleman, who learned to ski in his seventies, can manage those curves.

The quality of the snow is legendary. As the Pacific storms roll in across the province from the west, they dump the most amazing soft blanket on Sovereign Lakes, day after sublime winter day. When the humidity rises, a cool mist coats the stunted alpine firs, resulting in weird and wonderful snow ghosts.

Downhill skiing is a great sport, as is backcountry touring. But cross-country skiing is something you can do your entire life. Just ask Jackrabbit Johannsen. And when I look around this facility, at the national teams from half a dozen countries training as hard as they can alongside the local yokels up for another day in paradise, I am simply inspired.

Partway down the Lars Taylor trail is the Black Prince Cabin, a funky little log structure that serves as a warming hut for skiers. Volunteers start a fire in the massive wood stove each morning, and by the time we get there, the first logs have burned down to coals. We top them up, pull out the thermos of tea, and warm our hands over the crackling fire.

Lester Kelly, nonagenarian cross-country skier, at Sovereign Lake (photo courtesy of the McDonald collection)

And we start planning. For next year. The first spring hike. A new paddling adventure. Where will we find the best Pinot Noir? When will the meadowlarks return? Our plans remind me of something I once heard from Dasho Kinley Dorji, the secretary of the Ministry of Information and Communications in Bhutan. He stressed the importance of taking time for an "interlude" instead of racing around all the time—a chance to look around, slow down, take stock of what really makes you happy.

"Give yourself that gift from time to time," he said. Coming from a country where they measure GNH (Gross National Happiness) rather than GNP (Gross National Product), he must know what he's talking about.

Sovereign Lake Nordic Centre
250 Sovereign Lake Road
Vernon, BC

Recipes

Heirloom Tomato Gazpacho

Courtesy of Jeff Van Geest, Executive Chef, Miradoro at Tinhorn Creek

SERVES 6

2 lb (approx. 1 kg) very ripe heirloom tomatoes
1 large sweet onion (preferably something like a Walla Walla or Vidalia)
4 cloves garlic (the good kind you get from farmers' markets)
½ cup (115 g) basil leaves
½ cup (115 g) parsley leaves
¼ cup (55 g) mint leaves
1 cup (250 mL) extra-virgin olive oil
½ cup (125 mL) white wine vinegar
kosher salt and fresh cracked black pepper, to taste

Roughly chop tomatoes, onion, and garlic. Place in a bowl, then combine with remaining ingredients. Let mixture marinate overnight in the refrigerator.

The next day, pulse the mixture in a food processor until a uniform, slightly coarse texture is achieved. Season to taste with salt and pepper.

Serve cold in chilled bowls and garnish with good extra-virgin olive oil and croutons.

Heirloom tomatoes

Squash heaven

Heirloom Tomato Gazpacho

Courtesy of Thomas Render, Executive Chef, Naramata Heritage Inn

SERVES 6

1 English cucumber, peeled and seeded
2 red peppers, seeded and sliced
12 large heirloom tomatoes, cut into wedges
1 sweet onion, peeled and sliced thinly
½ cup (125 mL) extra-virgin olive oil
juice from 1 lemon
½ cup (115 g) fresh basil
2 cups (500 mL) water

In a non-reactive bowl, combine all ingredients. Place bowl in the refrigerator and leave overnight.

The next day, transfer the mixture to a blender and blend until smooth. Season to taste with salt. If a spicier gazpacho is desired, add a jalapeno pepper. Serve chilled. Grilled spot prawns are a great garnish, along with fresh herbs.

Purée of Carrot and Roasted Poblano Pepper with Coconut Milk Soup

Courtesy of Mark Ashton, Executive Chef, Lake Breeze Vineyards

SERVES 8

2 large poblano peppers
1 medium onion (⅓ lb [150 g]), coarsely chopped
1 heaping Tbsp (20 g) chopped garlic
1 large potato (½ lb [225 g])
3 lb (1.4 kg) freshly picked carrots, peeled and coarsely chopped
1 14-oz (398 mL) tin coconut milk
1 quart (1 L) chicken or vegetable stock
½ cup (115 g) coarsely chopped Italian or flat-leaf parsley
salt and white pepper, to taste

Roast poblanos over an open flame, on the barbecue, or under the broiler until blackened. Cool, peel, seed, and coarsely chop.

In a large pot over low heat, sweat the onion, poblanos, and garlic until onion is soft and translucent, approximately 10 to 15 minutes.

Add potato, carrots, coconut milk, stock, and parsley to the pot. Cover and let simmer for approximately 40 minutes, or until carrots are soft.

Purée in a blender until smooth, then strain. Season with salt and white pepper and serve warm.

Purée of Carrot and Roasted Poblano Pepper with Coconut Milk Soup

Spot Prawn Salad with Prosciutto and Raspberries

Courtesy of Elephant Island Orchard Wines

SERVES 6

1 cup (250 mL) Elephant Island Little King sparkling wine

1 lb (450 g) spot prawns, shell on

⅓ cup (75 mL) olive oil

1 pint (220 g) fresh raspberries, divided

1 small shallot, minced

1 Tbsp (15 g) chopped fresh Italian parsley

2 slices prosciutto

generous pinches of sea salt

4 to 6 cups (440–660 g) baby spinach, or 1 head butter
  lettuce, torn into small pieces

Pour wine into a saucepan and bring to a boil. Add prawns—don't worry if they aren't all submerged. Reduce heat to low, cover pan, and barely simmer, stirring occasionally, until prawns are cooked through, 2 to 3 minutes. Strain prawns and reserve liquid. Cool prawns in an ice bath or under cold running water, then peel. Refrigerate until ready to use.

Pour cooking liquid back into the saucepan and bring to a boil. Stir often, until liquid has thickened and measures about ¼ cup (60 mL). Watch carefully and lower heat, if necessary, toward the end to prevent burning.

For the dressing, place reduced cooking liquid, olive oil, ¼ cup (60 g) raspberries, shallot, and parsley in a blender. Whirl to purée, then strain half the dressing through a fine sieve to remove the seeds. Pour into a small bowl. If making ahead, cover and refrigerate for up to 3 days. Pour remaining dressing into a large bowl.

For the salad, lightly coat a small frying pan with olive oil and heat over medium. Add prosciutto and fry, turning occasionally, until crisp, 3 to 4 minutes. Remove and drain on paper towel. Toss prawns with unstrained dressing and pinches of salt. Let stand at room temperature to marinate, about 15 minutes. Add spinach and remaining raspberries to prawns. Drizzle with strained dressing, then toss to coat evenly. Divide and arrange on salad plates and crumble prosciutto overtop.

Chef's trick: Add a handful of fresh parsley leaves to the salad as a flavour booster!

Red Wine Vinegar, Fresh Dill, and Soft Unripened Goat Cheese Dressing

Courtesy of The Vinegar Works

MAKES ½ CUP (125 ML)

¼ cup (60 g) soft unripened goat cheese (chèvre or feta), crumbled
2 Tbsp (30 mL) red wine vinegar
2 Tbsp (30 mL) olive oil
1 Tbsp (15 g) finely chopped fresh dill
1 Tbsp (15 g) finely chopped parsley
salt and freshly ground pepper, to taste

In a 1-cup (250 mL) jar, combine cheese and vinegar until smooth. If using feta, this might take a bit of work, or if the feta is fairly dry, it may not be rendered entirely smooth. That's okay. It doesn't have to be perfectly smooth.

Mix in olive oil until blended.

Add dill, parsley, salt, and pepper. Add more oil or vinegar, or milk or water, if the consistency of the finished dressing is too thick for your liking. This dressing can be used either thick or thin. Thick, it makes a great dip or spread for crackers or bread. It also makes a great alternative to mayo in a sandwich. Thin, it can be drizzled on beets or other vegetables or simply used to dress a salad. This dressing will keep for several days in the refrigerator if you don't overindulge and devour it in one sitting.

Lobster Pasta

Courtesy of Ricardo's Mediterranean Kitchen and from the book *That's Amore*

SERVES 4

4 to 5 field mushrooms, sliced
8 cloves garlic, cut into small cubes and roasted
1 cup (225 g) langoustine lobster meat (or substitute 10 prawns)
1 oz (30 mL) white wine
1 Tbsp (15 g) butter
10 spears fresh asparagus
pinches of dried parsley, chili powder, salt, and pepper
8 oz (225 g) linguine noodles (½ package), cooked al dente
¼ cup (60 mL) extra-virgin olive oil
1 ripe Roma tomato, cubed
1 Tbsp (15 g) freshly grated Parmesan cheese

In a medium pan, sauté mushrooms, roasted garlic, and lobster meat with the wine and a drizzle of olive oil.

Add butter, asparagus, parsley, chili powder, and salt and pepper. Continue to sauté.

Remove pan from heat. Add noodles and olive oil, and toss to mix.

Add tomato, then season to taste with more salt and pepper.

Place pasta on plates, and top with Parmesan cheese.

Chili-Rubbed Prawn Wrap

Courtesy of Frog City Café

SERVES 6

36 shelled prawns
1 Tbsp (15 g) butter
6 cloves garlic
chili powder, to taste

1 cup (250 mL) sour cream
3 Tbsp (45 mL) lime juice (from 1 whole lime)
½ bunch cilantro, chopped
1 tsp (5 g) salt
1 tsp (5 g) chili powder
3 cloves garlic, minced

6 large spinach tortillas
grated mozzarella cheese
diced tomatoes
sliced avocado
shredded red cabbage
shredded green lettuce

In a large frying pan over medium heat, sauté prawns with butter and garlic. Sprinkle prawns with chili powder and cook for approximately 5 minutes, or until prawns are done.

To make the dressing, combine sour cream, lime juice, cilantro, salt, chili powder, and garlic in a bowl. Set aside until ready to make wraps.

Grill or heat up tortillas. On one third of each wrap, spread desired amount of dressing, warm prawns, mozzarella, tomatoes, avocado, red cabbage, and lettuce. Fold in the sides of the tortillas, then roll tightly to create wraps.

Potato, Ham, and Village Alpine Meadow (Swiss) Gratin

Courtesy of The Village Cheese Company

SERVES 6

2 lb (approx. 1 kg) baking potatoes, thinly sliced (about 6 cups [1.5 L])
1 large onion, finely chopped
6 oz (170 g) thinly sliced cooked ham
1¼ cups (310 mL) chicken broth
2 Tbsp (30 g) all-purpose flour
2 cups (220 g) shredded Village Alpine Meadow (Swiss) cheese

Preheat oven to 375°F (190°C). In a 2-quart (2 L) shallow rectangular baking dish, layer half of the potato slices and half the onion. Sprinkle with salt and pepper.

Arrange ham slices evenly over potatoes and onion.

Top with a second layer of potatoes and onion. Sprinkle with salt and pepper.

In a saucepan, combine chicken broth and flour until smooth. Cook and stir over medium-high heat until mixture boils and thickens; pour over potatoes, onion, and ham in baking dish. Sprinkle cheese evenly over surface.

Bake, uncovered, for 60 to 70 minutes, or until potatoes are tender and cheese is browned. Let stand 5 minutes before cutting and serving.

Roast Duck Breast with Blackberry-Plum Compote and Sautéed Red Beets

Courtesy of Bruno Terroso, Executive Chef, Vanilla Pod at Poplar Grove Winery

SERVES 4

1 cup (225 g) blackberries
1 cup (225 g) chopped red-fleshed plums (Oxheart or June Blood)
2 Tbsp (30 g) sugar
2 oz (60 mL) Poplar Grove Syrah

2 Tbsp (30 mL) extra-virgin olive oil
4 red beet roots, parcooked, peeled, and sliced
4 beet tops, washed and chopped
2 Tbsp (30 mL) balsamic vinegar

4 duck breasts
salt and pepper, to taste

In a saucepan over high heat, combine blackberries, plums, sugar, and Syrah. Cover and simmer for 15 minutes, stirring occasionally. Compote should be the consistency of a loose jam. Set aside and keep warm.

In a pan over high heat, heat olive oil and add the sliced beet roots and beet tops. Sauté until tops start to wilt and beet roots are hot. To finish, deglaze with balsamic vinegar and season with salt and pepper.

Preheat oven to 400°F (200°C). Trim excess fat off the duck breasts and score skin. Season each duck breast with salt and pepper. Render duck, skin sides down, until crispy (start in cold pan over low heat, draining excess fat every 1 to 2 minutes).

Once the skin is crispy, flip the breasts over to sear the rest of the breast. Next, place the duck breasts in a pan and roast in the oven for approximately 3 to 5 minutes. The duck should be cooked to a temperature of medium rare.

To serve, place the beet roots and tops in the centre of each plate. Thinly slice each duck breast; fan one breast over beets on each plate. Top with compote and serve.

Balaton Sour Cherry Pie with Lavender

Courtesy of Doug Matthias, Forest Green Man Lavender Farm

SERVES 6

1 recipe pie crust dough
1 cup plus 1 Tbsp (240 g) sugar, divided
3 Tbsp (45 g) cornstarch (see Chef's trick)
¼ tsp (1 g) salt
5 cups (about 2 lb [1 kg]) whole pitted sour cherries
1 tsp (5 mL) fresh lemon juice
2 Tbsp (30 g) unsalted butter (¼ stick), cut into ½-inch
    (1 cm) cubes
1 Tbsp (10 g) chopped culinary lavender buds
1 Tbsp (15 mL) milk
vanilla ice cream (optional)

Make your favourite pie crust (enough for two 12-inch [30.5 cm] rounds) and let stand at least 1 hour.

Position rack in lower third of oven and preheat to 425°F (220°C). In a medium bowl, whisk 1 cup (225 g) of the sugar, cornstarch, and salt to blend. Stir in cherries and lemon juice; set aside.

Roll out half of the dough on a floured surface to create a 12-inch (30.5 cm) round. Transfer to a 9-inch (23 cm) glass pie dish. Trim dough overhang to ½ inch (1 cm). Roll out remaining dough on a floured surface to create another 12-inch (30.5 cm) round. Using a large knife or pastry wheel with a fluted edge, cut round into ten ¾-inch

(2 cm) -wide strips. Transfer filling to the dough-lined dish, mounding slightly in centre. Dot with butter and sprinkle lavender buds evenly overtop. Arrange dough strips atop filling, forming a lattice; trim dough strip overhang to ½ inch (1 cm). Fold bottom crust up over ends of strips and crimp edges to seal. Brush lattice crust (not edges) with milk. Sprinkle lattice with remaining 1 Tbsp (15 g) sugar.

Place pie on a rimmed baking sheet and bake 15 minutes. Reduce oven temperature to 375°F (190°C). Bake pie for up to 1 additional hour, until filling is bubbling and crust is golden brown. Cover the edges with foil if browning too quickly. Transfer pie to a metal rack and allow to cool completely. Cut into wedges and serve with vanilla ice cream and Black Widow Pinot Gris, 2010 vintage.

Chef's trick: As an alternative to thickening with cornstarch, pit the cherries, mix with the sugar, and let stand overnight. Drain liquid into a saucepan and reduce until thick. Place the cherries in the pie crust, pour the reduced liquid overtop, add the top crust, and bake normally. This system also works well for rhubarb pie!

Balaton sour cherries

Rhubarb Custard Pie

Courtesy of Erna Kelly

SERVES 6

½ cup (60 g) flour
¼ cup (50 g) brown sugar
¼ cup (55 g) butter
½ tsp (2.5 g) cinnamon, or to taste

3 eggs
1¼ cups (280 g) sugar
2 Tbsp (30 g) flour
3 cups (675 g) finely chopped rhubarb, fresh from the
    garden
1 unbaked pie crust

Preheat oven to 450°F (230°C).

To make topping, combine flour, brown sugar, butter, and cinnamon in a small bowl. Set aside.

In a medium bowl, beat the eggs until frothy. Mix sugar and flour; add to the eggs. Then add the rhubarb. Mix well and pour into unbaked pie crust. Crumble the topping mixture overtop of the filling. Bake for 10 minutes, then reduce temperature to 350°F (175°C) and bake for an additional 35 to 40 minutes.

Cherry Chocolate Mousse

Courtesy of Okanagan Spirits

SERVES 4

3 egg yolks
⅓ cup (75 mL) stock syrup (see Chef's trick)
⅙ cup (40 mL) Okanagan Spirits sour cherry liqueur
3.5 oz (100 g) cherries, finely chopped
5.5 oz (155 g) dark chocolate (72 percent cocoa solids),
    melted
1½ cups (375 mL) double cream

Combine the egg yolks, ⅓ of the stock syrup, and ¼ of the sour cherry liqueur in a bowl. Place over a pan of gently simmering water (make sure the water doesn't touch the base or sides of the bowl) and whisk continuously until the mixture thickens, turns frothy, and forms a sabayon.

Meanwhile, heat the remaining stock syrup in a saucepan over medium heat until it reaches 250°F (120°C). Place the sabayon in a food mixer and quickly whisk in the warm stock syrup until the entire mixture is cold. Mix in the chopped cherries and the remaining liqueur.

Fold in the melted chocolate and the double cream, and mix until smooth. Transfer the mousse into moulds and put in the refrigerator to set for 2 hours.

Chef's trick: To make stock syrup, place ⅙ cup (38 g) sugar and ⅙ cup (40 mL) water in a saucepan over medium heat; cook until mixture reaches 250°F (120°C).

Blueberry Orange Cake

Courtesy of Rogers Foods

SERVES 20

2 cups (220 g) Rogers All-Purpose Flour
1 Tbsp (15 g) baking powder
1 tsp (5 g) salt
¾ cup (170 g) sugar
¼ tsp (1 g) nutmeg
⅔ cup (150 g) butter
2 eggs
¾ cup (175 mL) milk
1½ cups (340 g) fresh or frozen blueberries
¼ cup (55 g) sugar
¼ tsp (1 g) cinnamon

2 Tbsp (30 g) cornstarch
½ cup (115 g) sugar
¾ cup (175 mL) frozen orange juice concentrate
1½ cups (375 mL) water
1 Tbsp (15 mL) orange-flavoured liqueur, such as Grand Marnier (optional)

Preheat the oven to 350°F (175°C).

In a medium bowl, combine flour, baking powder, salt, sugar, and nutmeg; mix thoroughly. Cut in butter until mixture resembles coarse crumbs.

In a small bowl, beat eggs and milk together. Lightly stir into dry ingredients.

Toss blueberries in 2 Tbsp (30 g) flour or cinnamon sugar. Gently fold the blueberries into the batter. (Frozen blueberries will make a thicker batter.)

Spread batter into a greased 9 × 9-inch (23 × 23 cm) cake pan. Mix together sugar and cinnamon. Sprinkle overtop of cake. Bake for 40 to 50 minutes, or until a tester comes out clean.

Meanwhile, make the orange sauce. In a saucepan, combine cornstarch and sugar; mix well. Stir in orange juice and water. Cook over medium heat, stirring frequently until sauce thickens. Add orange liqueur to the sauce just before serving with warm cake.

Cherry Chocolate Mousse

Okanagan Valley Wineries

3 Mile Estate Winery
1465 Naramata Road
Penticton, BC
www.3milewinery.com

8th Generation Vineyard
6807 Highway 97
Summerland, BC
www.8thgeneration.com

**Antelope Ridge Estate
Winery**
32057 Road 13
Oliver, BC

Arrowleaf Cellars
1574 Camp Road
Winfield, BC
www.arrowleafcellars.com

Black Hills Estate Winery
4318 Black Sage Road
Oliver, BC
www.blackhillswinery.com

Black Widow Winery
1630 Naramata Road
Penticton, BC
www.blackwidowwinery.com

Blasted Church Vineyards
378 Parsons Road
Okanagan Falls, BC
www.blastedchurch.com

Blue Mountain Vineyard
2385 Allendale Road
Okanagan Falls, BC
www.bluemountainwinery.com

Bonitas Winery
20623 McDougald Road
Summerland, BC
www.bonitaswinery.com

**Burrowing Owl Estate
Winery**
500 Burrowing Owl Place
Oliver, BC
www.bovwine.ca

Calona Vineyards
1125 Richter Street
Kelowna, BC
www.calonavineyards.ca

Camelot Vineyards
3489 East Kelowna Road
Kelowna, BC
www.camelotvineyards.ca

Carriage House Wines
32764 Black Sage Road
Oliver, BC

Cassini Cellars
4828 Highway 97
Oliver, BC
www.cassini.ca

**Castoro de Oro Estate
Winery**
4004 Highway 97
Oliver, BC
www.castorodeoro.com

CedarCreek Estate Winery
5445 Lakeshore Road
Kelowna, BC
www.cedarcreek.bc.ca

Covert Farms Estate Winery
38614 107th Street
Oliver, BC
www.covertfarms.ca

**Coyote Bowl Church &
State Wines**
31120 87th Street
Oliver, BC
www.churchandstatewines.com

D'Angelo Estate Winery
979 Lochore Road
Penticton, BC
www.dangelowinery.com

Desert Hills Estate Winery
30480 71st Street
Oliver, BC
www.deserthills.ca

Dirty Laundry Vineyard
7311 Fiske Street
Summerland, **BC**
www.dirtylaundry.ca

Elephant Island Orchard Wines
2730 Aikins Loop
Naramata, **BC**
www.elephantislandwine.com

Ex Nihilo Vineyards
1525 Camp Road
Lake Country, **BC**
www.exnihilovineyards.com

Fairview Cellars
989 Cellar Road
Oliver, **BC**
www.fairviewcellars.ca

Gehringer Brothers Estate Winery
13166 326th Avenue (Road 8)
Oliver, **BC**
www.gehringerwines.ca

Gray Monk Estate Winery
1055 Camp Road
Lake Country, **BC**
www.graymonk.com

Greata Ranch Estate Winery
697 Highway 97
Peachland, **BC**
www.greataranchwinery.com

Hainle Vineyards and Deep Creek Estate Winery
5355 Trepanier Bench Road
Peachland, **BC**
www.hainle.com

Heaven's Gate Estate Winery
8001 Happy Valley Road
Summerland, **BC**
www.heavensgatewinery.ca

Hester Creek Estate Winery
877 Road 8
Oliver, **BC**
www.hestercreek.com

Hidden Chapel Winery
482 Pinehill Road
Oliver, **BC**
www.hiddenchapelwinery.com

Hillside Estate Winery
1350 Naramata Road
Penticton, **BC**
www.hillsidewinery.ca

Hollywood and Wine Winery
9819 Lumsden Avenue
Summerland, **BC**

House of Rose Winery
2270 Garner Road
Kelowna, **BC**
www.houseofrose.ca

Howling Bluff Estate Wines
1086 Three Mile Road
Penticton, **BC**
www.howlingbluff.ca

Inniskillin Okanagan Estate Winery
32074 123rd Street
Oliver, **BC**
www.inniskillin.com

Jackson-Triggs Okanagan Estate
7857 Tucelnuit Drive
Oliver, **BC**
www.jacksontriggswinery.com

JoieFarm Winery
2825 Naramata Road
Naramata, **BC**
www.joiefarm.com

Kalala Organic Estate Winery
3361 Glencoe Road
West Kelowna, **BC**
www.kalalawines.ca

Kettle Valley Winery
2988 Hayman Road
Naramata, **BC**
www.kettlevalleywinery.com

Krāzē Legz Vineyard and Winery
141 Fir Avenue
Kaleden, **BC**
www.krazelegz.com

La Frenz Winery
1525 Randolph Road
Penticton, **BC**
www.lafrenzwinery.com

Lake Breeze Vineyards
930 Sammet Road
Naramata, **BC**
www.lakebreeze.ca

Lang Vineyards
2493 Gammon Road
Naramata, **BC**
www.langvineyards.ca

La Stella Winery
8123 148th Avenue, RR2
Osoyoos, **BC**
www.lastella.ca

Laughing Stock Vineyards
1548 Naramata Road
Penticton, **BC**
www.laughingstock.ca

Liquidity Wines
4720 Allendale Road
Okanagan Falls, **BC**
www.liquiditywines.com

Little Straw Vineyards
2815 Ourtoland Road
Kelowna, **BC**
www.littlestraw.bc.ca

Meyer Family Vineyards
4287 McLean Creek Road
Okanagan Falls, **BC**
www.mfvwines.com

Misconduct Wine Co.
375 Upper Bench Road North
Penticton, **BC**
www.misconductwineco.com

Mission Hill Winery
1730 Mission Hill Road
West Kelowna, **BC**
www.missionhillwinery.com

Mistral Estate Winery
250 Upper Bench Road
Penticton, **BC**

Monster Vineyards
1010 Tupper Avenue
Penticton, **BC**
www.monstervineyards.com

Moon Curser Vineyards
3628 Highway 3 East
Osoyoos, **BC**
www.mooncurser.com

Moraine Estate Winery
1865 Naramata Road
Penticton, **BC**
www.morainewinery.com

Mt. Boucherie Winery
829 Douglas Road
West Kelowna, **BC**
www.mtboucheriewinery.com

Nichol Vineyard
1285 Smethurst Road
Naramata, **BC**
www.nicholvineyard.com

Nk'Mip Cellars Winery
1400 Rancher Creek Road
Osoyoos, **BC**
www.nkmipcellars.com

Noble Ridge Vineyard & Winery
2320 Oliver Ranch Road
Okanagan Falls, **BC**
www.nobleridge.com

Oliver Twist Estate Winery
398 Lupine Lane
Oliver, **BC**
www.olivertwistwinery.com

Painted Rock Estate Winery
400 Smythe Drive
Penticton, **BC**
www.paintedrock.ca

Pentâge Winery
4400 Lakeside Road
Penticton, **BC**
www.pentage.com

Perseus Winery
134 Lower Bench Road
Penticton, **BC**
perseuswinery.com

Platinum Bench Estate Winery
4102 Black Sage Road
Oliver, **BC**
www.platinumbench.com

Poplar Grove Winery
425 Middle Bench Road North
Penticton, **BC**
www.poplargrove.ca

Quails' Gate Winery
3303 Boucherie Road
West Kelowna, **BC**
www.quailsgate.com

Quinta Ferreira Estate Winery
6094 Black Sage Road
Oliver, **BC**
www.quintaferreira.com

Red Rooster Winery
891 Naramata Road
Penticton, **BC**
www.redroosterwinery.com

River Stone Estate Winery
143 Buchanan Road
Oliver, **BC**
www.riverstoneestatewinery.ca

Road 13 Vineyards
799 Ponderosa Road, Road 13
Oliver, **BC**
www.road13vineyards.com

Rollingdale Winery
2306 Hayman Road
West Kelowna, **BC**
www.rollingdale.ca

Rustico Winery
4444 Kobau Road
Oliver, **BC**
www.rusticowinery.com

St. Hubertus Estate Winery
5225 Lakeshore Road
Kelowna, **BC**
www.st-hubertus.bc.ca

See Ya Later Ranch
2575 Green Lake Road
Okanagan Falls, **BC**
www.sylranch.com

Serendipity Winery
990 Debeck Road
Naramata, **BC**
serendipitywinery.com

Silkscarf Winery
4917 Gartrell Road
Summerland, **BC**
www.silkw.net

Silver Sage Winery
32032-87th Avenue
Oliver, **BC**
www.silversagewinery.com

Sleeping Giant Fruit Winery
6206 Canyon View Road
Summerland, **BC**
www.sleepinggiantfruitwinery.ca

Sonoran Estate Winery
5716 Gartrell Road
Summerland, **BC**
www.sonoranwinery.com

Stag's Hollow Winery
2237 Sun Valley Way
Okanagan Falls, **BC**
www.stagshollowwinery.com

Stoneboat Vineyards
356 Orchard Grove Road
Oliver, **BC**
www.stoneboatvineyards.com

Stonehill Estate Winery
170 Upper Bench Road
Penticton, **BC**

Sumac Ridge Estate Winery
17403 Highway 97
Summerland, **BC**
www.sumacridge.com

Summerhill Pyramid Winery
4870 Chute Lake Road
Kelowna, **BC**
www.summerhill.bc.ca

Synchromesh Wines
4220 McLean Creek Road
Okanagan Falls, **BC**
www.synchromeshwines.ca

Tangled Vines Estate Winery
2140 Sun Valley Way
Okanagan Falls, **BC**
www.tangledvineswinery.com

Tantalus Vineyards
1670 Dehart Road
Kelowna, **BC**
www.tantalus.ca

Terravista Vineyards
1853 Sutherland Road
Penticton, **BC**
www.terravistavineyards.com

Therapy Vineyards
940 Lower Debeck Road
Naramata, **BC**
www.therapyvineyards.com

Thornhaven Estate Winery
6816 Andrew Avenue
Summerland, **BC**
www.thornhaven.com

Tinhorn Creek Vineyards
32830 Tinhorn Creek Road
Oliver, **BC**
www.tinhorn.com

Township 7 Vineyards & Winery
1450 McMillan Avenue
Penticton, **BC**
www.township7.com

Upper Bench Estate Winery
170 Upper Bench Road South
Penticton, **BC**
www.upperbench.ca

Van Westen Vineyards
2800A Aikins Loop
Naramata, **BC**
www.vanwestenvineyards.com

Volcanic Hills Estate Winery
2845 Boucherie Road
West Kelowna, **BC**
www.volcanichillswinery.com

Wild Goose Vineyards
2145 Sun Valley Way
Okanagan Falls, **BC**
www.wildgoosewinery.com

Working Horse Winery
5266 Coldham Road
Peachland, **BC**

Young & Wyse Winery
9503 12th Avenue
Osoyoos, **BC**
www.youngandwysewine.com

Okanagan Valley Farmers' Markets

Osoyoos Market on Main
Town Hall Square, Main Street, Osoyoos
Saturdays 8:00 AM–1:00 PM, from May long weekend
through September
The market offers a buffet of multicultural, agricultural,
bakery, and artisanal choices.

Oliver Country Market A-Fair
Lion's Park, Oliver
Saturdays 8:30 AM–12:30 PM, from June to October
The small country market has partnered with the Regional
District of Okanagan-Similkameen to help provide local
produce, baking, honey, and crafts of the highest quality.

Penticton Farmers' Market
100 Block Main Street, Penticton
Saturdays 8:30 AM–noon and Tuesdays 4:30–8:30 PM, from
May to October
The producers' catchment area for the farm-fresh fruits and
vegetables, garlic and other spices, honey, eggs, and flowers
includes the South Okanagan and the fertile Similkameen
Valley, with its emphasis on organic farming methods.
Vendors selling at the market must produce what they sell,
and the market prides itself on providing locally grown
produce.

Naramata Community Market
Wharf Park, Naramata
Wednesdays 3:30–6:30 PM, from start of June to early
September
Residents and visitors are invited to enjoy fresh fruits and
vegetables, delicious prepared foods, and unique crafts.

Summerland Country Market
Memorial Park, Wharton Street, Summerland
Tuesdays 9:00 AM–1:00 PM, from May to October
The Summerland farmers' market presents products from
local vendors—produce, preserves, and home-baked goods.

Peachland Farmers and Crafters Market
Heritage Park, Beach Avenue, Peachland
Sundays 10:00 AM–2:00 PM, from May through September
Started in 2006, this farmers and crafters market presents
a wide variety of vendors who all offer "made, baked, or
grown products," and a fantastic lake view.

Kelowna Farmers' and Crafters' Market
Corner of Dilworth Drive and Springfield Road, Kelowna
Wednesdays and Saturdays 8:00 AM–1:00 PM, from April
through October
This market offers a huge variety of farm products and
organic produce—jams, baking, meats, ethnic foods, soaps,

body products, flowers, plants—as well as concessions, entertainment, festivals, and much, much more.

Lake Country Farmers' Market
Swalwell Park, Bottom Wood Lake Road, Winfield
Fridays 3:00 PM–7:00 PM, from June to September
Local vendors selling a combination of fruit, vegetables, crafts, fresh breads, borscht, sausages, and wraps.

Vernon Farmers' Market
Kal Tire Place Parking Lot, 3445 43rd Avenue, Vernon
Mondays and Thursdays 8:00 AM–1:00 PM, from April through October
One of the oldest farm markets in the Okanagan, with over one hundred annual growers and artisans offering everything from fresh fruit, vegetables, and plants to handicrafts, eggs, and fresh-baked delicacies. Buskers and live entertainment, as well as Special Event Mondays every long weekend. Acres of free parking.

Vernon Friday Night Farmers' Market
4900 27th Street, Vernon
Fridays 3:00 PM–7:00 PM, from May to October
Vernon's best homegrown vegetables and berries, eggs, baked goods, and crafts, plus food concessions and entertainment.

Armstrong Farmers' Market
IPE Fairgrounds, 3371 Pleasant Valley Road, Armstrong
Saturdays 8:00 AM–noon, from end of April through October
This market has been in operation since 1973 and offers strong support for locally grown fresh fruit and vegetables, bedding plants, home-baked wholesome goods, honey, preserves, pottery, soaps, woodwork, and all kinds of quality handicrafts.

1. How Big Is the Valley?
¹ Gayton, Don. *Okanagan Odyssey*. Victoria, BC: Rocky Mountain Books, 2010, pg. 12.

9. Mahoney Lake Circuit
¹ Cannings, Dick. "A wild hawk chase to White Lake." Dick Cannings: Birds and Books, October 29, 2011. www.dickcannings.com.

16. Farmers' Market
¹ "Canned Goods," lyrics by Greg Brown.

26. 8th Generation and a Glass Full of Bubbles
¹ Gismondi, Anthony. Gismondi on Wine, July 20, 2010. www.gismondionwine.com.

28. Culinary Summerland
¹ Antoine de St. Exupéry was a French pilot and author.

31. Quails' Gate Winery
¹ Schreiner, John. John Schreiner on wine, November 10, 2011. www.johnschreiner.blogspot.ca.

34. Kelowna Wine
¹ Gismondi, Anthony. *The Vancouver Sun*, April 18, 2013.

Books

Cannings, Richard. *Roadside Nature Tours through the Okanagan*. Vancouver, BC: Greystone Books, 2009.

Cassano, Franco. *Modernizzare stanca* (Modernization is Tiring). Bologna: Il Mulino, 2001.

Gayton, Don. *Okanagan Odyssey*. Victoria, BC: Rocky Mountain Books, 2010.

Honoré, Carl. *In Praise of Slow*. Toronto: Vintage Canada Edition, 2004.

Kimbrell, Andres, ed. *Fatal Harvest: The Tragedy of Industrial Agriculture*. Washington, DC: Island Press, 2002.

Kundera, Milan. *Slowness*. New York: HarperCollins, 1995.

Langford, Dan, and Sandra Langford. *Cycling the Kettle Valley Railway*. Surrey, BC: Rocky Mountain Books, 2002.

MacLean, Natalie. *Red, White, and Drunk All Over*. Toronto, ON: Anchor Canada, 2007.

Parish, Roberta, Ray Coupé, and Dennis Lloyd. *Plants of Southern Interior British Columbia and the Inland Northwest*. Vancouver, BC: Lone Pine Publishing, 1996.

Petrini, Carlo. *Slow Food Nation*. New York: Rizzoli ex libris, 2005.

Petrini, Carlo. *Slow Food: The Case for Taste*. New York: Columbia University Press, 2001.

Visser, Margaret. *Much Depends on Dinner*. Toronto, ON: HarperCollins, 2008.

Websites

Slow Food Manifesto (www.slowfood.com)

INDEX

227